INFLUENTIAL
L!VES

HILLARY CLINTON

FORMER FIRST LADY AND SECRETARY OF STATE

ANNE C. CUNNINGHAM AND
JEFF BURLINGAME

Enslow Publishing
101 W. 23rd Street
Suite 240
New York, NY 10011
USA

enslow.com

Published in 2018 by Enslow Publishing, LLC.
101 W. 23rd Street, Suite 240, New York, NY 10011

Library of Congress Cataloging-in-Publication Data

Names: Cunningham, Anne C., author. | Burlingame, Jeff, author
Title: Hillary Clinton : former first lady and secretary of state / Anne C. Cunningham and Jeff Burlingame.
Description: New York : Enslow Publishing, 2018. | Series: Influential lives | Includes bibliographical references and index.
Identifiers: ISBN 9780766085015 (library-bound)
Subjects: LCSH: Clinton, Hillary Rodham—Juvenile literature. | Presidential candidates—United States—Biography—Juvenile literature. | Women presidential candidates—United States—Biography—Juvenile literature. | Cabinet officers—United States—Biography—Juvenile literature. | Women cabinet officers—United States—Biography—Juvenile literature. | United States. Department of State—Biography—Juvenile literature. | United States. Congress. Senate—Biography—Juvenile literature. | Legislators—United States—Biography—Juvenile literature. | Women legislators—United States—Biography—Juvenile literature. | Presidents' spouses—United States—Biography—Juvenile literature.
Classification: LCC E887.C55 S86 2018 | DDC 324.092 [B] —dc23

Printed in the United States of America

To Our Readers: We have done our best to make sure all websites in this book were active and appropriate when we went to press. However, the author and the publisher have no control over and assume no liability for the material available on those websites or on any websites they may link to. Any comments or suggestions can be sent by e-mail to customerservice@enslow.com.

Photo credits: Cover (inset), p. 1 Joseph Sohm/Shutterstock.com; p. 4 Wellesley College Archives/REUTERS/Newscom; p. 9 The Washington Post/Getty Images; p. 13 Clinton Press Office/UPI/Newscom; pp. 19, 28, 39 Wellesley College/Sygma/Getty Images; p. 23 Lee Balterman/The LIFE Picture Collection/Getty Images; p. 32 Boston Globe/Getty Images; p. 36 Bettmann/Getty Images; p. 44 ZUMA Press, Inc./Alamy Stock Photo; pp. 49, 59, 62, 82 © AP Images; p. 52, 62 Cynthia Johnson/The LIFE Images Collection/Getty Images; p. 56 CBS Photo Archive/Getty Images; p. 57 Brooks Kraft/Sygma/Getty Images; p. 73 Chris Hondros/Hulton Archive; p. 79 Stan Honda/AFP/Getty Images; p. 86 The White House/Getty Images; p. 91 Xinhua News Agency/Getty Images; pp. 96–97 Rick Friedman/Corbis News/Getty Images; pp. 98–99 NurPhoto/Getty Images; p. 104 Timothy A. Clary/AFP/Getty Images; back cover and interior pages background graphic zffoto/Shutterstock.com.

Contents

CHAPTER ONE

Graduation Speech

· · · · · · · · · ·

A s Hillary Rodham ascended to the podium, few in attendance at the Wellesley College Class of 1969 graduation ceremony knew exactly what to expect. Perhaps those who knew Hillary best were not surprised to hear her so forcefully articulate her generation's experience of an especially turbulent historic moment. While Hillary was known to speak her mind, in this circumstance, it was unusual for a student to speak at all. The nearly century-old Wellesley College typically did not let students give commencement speeches. In fact, college president Ruth Adams had to give the matter serious consideration before allowing it. She eventually assented to the wishes of the graduating class and allowed Hillary to prepare some remarks for the event. They ended up reverberating far past the town of Wellesley.

· ·

In 1969, Hillary Rodham became the first Wellesley student to deliver a commencement address. The speech earned her media attention.

It was no surprise the Class of 1969 had chosen the popular Hillary Rodham to be its speaker. In fact, no one else was considered. The college president later said, "There was no debate . . . as to who their spokesman was to be."[1] What she ended up saying made it a historic moment for many in her generation.

Contrasting Speeches

On graduation day, a dynamic United States senator spoke immediately before Hillary. He was the country's first-ever African American senator, Edward Brooke. Senator Brooke talked about the sometimes-violent protests young people were staging across America. At the time, the country was dealing with many divisive issues, including a highly unpopular war in Vietnam. Many college students protested the war and other actions they did not believe in. They often focused their anger on the government.

Senator Brooke told the graduates that protests were hurting the country rather than helping it.[2] He said many of the protesters were doing so "without purpose."[3] He said it was "a perversion of democratic privilege."[4] He believed the United States would be better off if the protests stopped. The senator wanted everyone to stand behind the government.

While she waited her turn to speak, Hillary grew frustrated by the senator's comments. She and her classmates were among those he was talking about. But Hillary felt protesting was important for her generation. She believed all Americans should be allowed to voice their opinions whenever they felt like it. She was also upset that the senator did not speak about any of the issues she and her classmates were concerned about. Years later, Hillary said the senator had talked as if everything was fine in the world. She knew it was not.[5] Popular leaders, such as Martin Luther King Jr., had recently been assassinated. America was fighting in an unpopular war. Minority groups, such as African Americans and women, were

Student Activism

The late 1960s were heydays of student activism. As the Baby Boomer generation was entering young adulthood, they rejecting en masse the conformity and conservatism marking the previous decade. Organizations such as Students for a Democratic Society (SDS) were founded on principles that came to be associated with the New Left. The New Left rejected a dogmatic Marxist focus on historical class struggle, choosing instead to confront social problems in a way that today might be called "intersectional." Likewise, the Student Non-Violent Coordinating Committee (SNCC) pursued racial justice and civil rights, organizing sit-ins and "freedom rides." In 1970, the National Guard opened fire on students at Kent State University, killing four and wounding nine others. The event placed a pall over student demonstrations and is recalled today as a tragic national embarrassment.

vying for equal rights. In many ways, the country was in turmoil. But the senator did not mention any of those issues in detail.

Hillary stayed up most of the night before graduation nervously writing her speech. Several friends helped her and offered suggestions. But when she heard Senator Brooke's comments she decided to change her plans at the last minute. After the college president introduced her to the crowd as "cheerful, good humored, good company, and a good friend to all of us,"[6] the twenty-one year-old Hillary stepped up to the microphone. She began with a response to the senator. Friends remember her speaking for ten minutes off the top of her head before finally beginning her prepared speech.[7]

> Protest is important and politicians should be trying to make what appears to be impossible, possible.

Senator Brooke had mentioned that 13.3 percent of Americans were living below the poverty line. He said this to make a point that the country had improved. During her speech, Hillary asked, "How can we talk about percentages and trends?"[8] She felt each person living in poverty was a human being and should not be treated as a number by a politician trying to make the government look good. She said there should be "respect between people where you don't see people as percentage points. Where you don't manipulate people."[9] She also said every protest is important and politicians should be trying to make "what appears to be impossible, possible."[10] Her speech was full of passion.

"She Will Probably Be the President of the United States Someday"

The crowd's reaction to her speech was mixed. The older people were embarrassed and shocked that a young woman would speak that way, especially in front of and about a United States senator. A mother of one graduate said, "I would have liked to have stopped her. I'm sure

Long before Hillary Clinton's career in politics began, a classmate predicted she would one day be president. Going into the 2016 election, many millions of Americans shared this opinion.

her mother would've liked to have stopped her. But her class absolutely encouraged her. And when she finished, they rose in a body and applauded her."[11]

One of those four hundred cheering classmates remembered Hillary's fiery speech. She said, "It was brash, it was brilliant, it was unplanned and it was disrespectful to Senator Brooke ... I can remember squirming in my seat. At the same time, the inner me was saying 'Alright!'"[12] Another classmate turned to her mother and said, "Take a good look at her. She will probably be the president of the United States someday."[13]

After the graduation ceremony, Hillary headed to a lake on campus. Swimming was not allowed, but she jumped in anyway. During the next few days, Hillary's speech became national news. Fighting for what she believed in—especially in opposition to a high-ranking politician—made an impact on her country. The graduation speech proved to be just the beginning for her. But at the end of an action-packed day in the spring of 1969, Hillary Rodham was not concerned with her future. All she wanted to do was go for a relaxing swim. So she did, on her terms.

CHAPTER TWO

Early Years

· · · · · · · · · · · · · · · · · ·

Hillary Diane Rodham was born in Chicago, Illinois, on October 26, 1947. By then, the city of Chicago had seen its share of ups and downs. In 1893, it famously hosted the World's Columbian Exposition, more commonly known as the World's Fair. This brought millions of visitors to the growing metropolis on the shore of Lake Michigan. Chicago would again be the site of this event forty years later. These World's Fairs are commemorated as two of the city flag's four stars. But conflict and tragedy visited the city, too. A fierce battle during the War of 1812 earned Chicago's flag another star, while a final star commemorates the Great Fire of 1871, which leveled miles of city buildings and left a third of the population homeless.[1]

The Great Fire also destroyed much of the grandeur Chicago's gritty residents had worked years to achieve. Its citizens were not defeated. Shortly after the fire, they turned their sorrow into inspiration. "Chicago" is an American Indian word meaning "strong" or "great,"[2] and its saddened residents were both. Following the fire, they rebuilt their city into one of the largest and most powerful in the United States. By 1900, 1.7 million people lived in Chicago.[3] When Hillary was born, the population had risen to 3.5 million.[4]

First-time parents Hugh and Dorothy Rodham were two of the city's residents. Hugh Rodham was a gruff thirty-six-year-old businessman from Pennsylvania. He was a former college football player and a navy officer during World War II. When Hillary was born, he owned and operated a small drapery business called Rodrik Fabrics. The window of his office looked out across the Chicago River.

Like many women of her era, Dorothy Rodham was a homemaker. She was born Dorothy Howell twenty-eight years earlier in the same Illinois city in which she gave birth to Hillary. By that time, the new mother already had lived a tumultuous life. Her parents were young when she was born and quickly proved unable to take care of her. So, at age eight, Dorothy and her three-year-old sister were sent to a small town in California to live with their strict grandparents. At fourteen, Dorothy left her grandparents' home and moved in with a local family. She worked full-time taking care of the family's children. After she finished high school, Dorothy returned to Chicago. She met Hugh Rodham there after applying for a job at a company he worked for. The couple married in 1942.

Hillary spent her first years living with her parents in a one-bedroom apartment. By the time she was

This 1950 portrait shows Hillary Rodham as a young girl. Hillary was raised to be tough and to stand up for herself, lessons she would draw from throughout her political career.

three, her parents had saved enough money to pay cash for a house in Park Ridge, an upper-middle-class suburb 15 miles (24 kilometers) north of Chicago. The family's two-story brick house on Wisner Street eventually became home to two more Rodham children: Hugh Jr., who was born three years after Hillary, and Anthony, who was born seven years after his big sister.

An Idyllic Childhood

Their children's well-being was a big reason the Rodhams picked Park Ridge. The suburb was known for its excellent schools, and education was very important to the Rodhams. The lifestyle there was much different than it was in Chicago. Hillary said, "[Park Ridge] was white and middle-class, a place where women stayed home to raise children while men commuted to work in the Loop, eighteen miles away. Many of the fathers took the train, but my dad had to make sales calls on potential customers, so he drove the family car to work every day."[5] Vanity may have been another reason her father chose to drive. Hugh Rodham's shiny Cadillac was one of his most prized possessions. He loved to show it off every chance he got.

The family's new neighborhood was full of children, including many boys. This helped Hillary learn to fight for what she wanted at an early age. Her mother said, "She was able to play with the boys and, yet, sort of earn their respect."[6] Occasionally that respect had to be earned physically. One day, Hillary came home crying after a neighbor girl beat her up. She did not receive any sympathy when she got there. Her mother used the opportunity to teach her a lesson. She sent her back out to fight the girl. Hillary did, and the bullying stopped.

Hillary's favorite childhood memories were the summer car trips her family took to her father's home state of Pennsylvania. Hillary's grandfather owned a cottage in the Pocono Mountains there. Hillary spent her days swimming in Lake Winola and exploring the tree-lined area surrounding the lake. Hillary said, "Those vacations were a big part of my childhood, not least because they provided some of the best times I ever had with my dad."[7]

Hillary was not only active during the summer, she was very involved year-round. She was a Brownie and, later, a Girl Scout and was considered a tomboy. She enjoyed riding her bike, playing softball and kickball, and traveling with her parents to Chicago to watch Cubs baseball games at historic Wrigley Field.

To most of the Park Ridge families, religion was as important as recreation. The Rodhams attended the First United Methodist Church. Hugh Rodham, in particular, was a devout Christian. Hillary said he "prayed kneeling by the side of his bed every night."[8] Dorothy Rodham taught Sunday school at the church. Her three children were among her students.

Outside of church, Hugh Rodham was a gruff man and a strict father. He had high expectations for his children. He expected them to work hard, just as he did. He often taught them tough real-life lessons about what could happen if they did not. Hillary said he would drive the family "down to skid row to see what became of people who, as he saw it, lacked the self-discipline and motivation to keep their lives on track."[9] It is easy to

15

understand why hard work was so important to Hillary's parents. Both had grown up during America's Great Depression, an era where money was scarce and jobs were hard to find. Families had to conserve to survive. Living through that time affected people's behavior long after the Depression ended in 1941.

The Rodham children were taught the value of hard work by being made to do it. The family was surviving just fine, but the children still were not handed what they wanted. "My parents gave me my belief in working hard, doing well in school and not being limited by the fact that I was a little girl," Hillary said.[10] "It really was the classic parenting situation, where the mother is the encourager and helper, and the father brings news from the outside world."[11]

> My parents gave me my belief in working hard, doing well in school and not being limited by the fact that I was a little girl.

Meeting her parents' high education standards was no problem for studious Hillary. She had little trouble getting good grades. Yet her tough father always pushed her to do better. Once, when Hillary brought home a report card with straight A's from junior high school, her hard-to-please father told the happy student, "Well, Hillary, that must be an easy school you go to."[12] Hillary was disappointed at her father's reaction, but she later said words like that from her father inspired her to work even harder.

Hugh Rodham's political beliefs also impacted Hillary. She said her father was "an old-fashioned Republican,

The Two-Party System

The two dominant political parties in the United States today are the Republicans and the Democrats. In a nutshell, Republicans tend to be pro-business and are religiously conservative. They support limited federal government involvement and are opposed to social entitlements. Democrats have drawn support from the working classes and minorities. They believe the government should be involved in fixing society's ills.

It is not unusual for Americans to become disaffected by their political party and change allegiance, like Hillary Clinton did in her youth, as the Republican and Democratic parties have naturally evolved.

In contrast to the United States, most democratic countries have more than two parties. Many Americans have called for an alternative viable third party to represent the values and concerns that both major parties of the government fail to address. But since losing parties in US elections don't stand to gain anything, there is little incentive to form and develop third parties. It is generally agreed that a third party candidate could never win a US presidential election. In modern history, third-party presidential candidates have not won any electoral votes, a track record that discourages third parties from suppporting and running serious candidates.

who, until he met Bill Clinton, eagerly pulled the 'R' [Republican] lever in every voting booth he ever entered."[13]

First Political Steps

Hillary became involved in politics at a young age. The 1960 presidential election hooked her. That year, a Democrat, John F. Kennedy, was elected president of the United States. A number of people felt illegal votes had helped Kennedy win. Hillary and a friend decided to help Republicans do something about it. The two thirteen-year-old girls hopped a bus from Park Ridge to downtown Chicago to visit addresses voters had listed on their registrations. They were checking to see if they actually lived where they said they did. Hillary said she was dropped off in a poor neighborhood and told to "knock on doors and ask people their names."[14] She discovered some of voters did not live at the addresses they had listed. That was illegal.

Hillary returned home and told her father what she had done. She thought he would be proud because he was one of those who thought Kennedy had stolen the election. But Hugh Rodham was not proud. Instead, he was upset his teenage daughter had traveled to Chicago without an adult. Hillary said, "He went nuts."[15]

That year, Hillary also got her first summer job. She worked for the Park Ridge Park District watching over a small playground near her house. Hillary said, "I pulled a wagon filled with balls, bats, jump ropes and other supplies back and forth. From that year on, I always had a summer job and often worked during the year."[16]

On May 5, 1961, astronaut Alan Shepard became the first American to travel into space. Many Americans were inspired by the man's courage to do something only one other person had done. Hillary was inspired, too. She wrote to the National Aeronautics and Space Administration (NASA) saying she, too, would like to be an astronaut. NASA's response was not very encouraging. The agency wrote back and said it did not accept girls into its space program. Hillary was devastated. She said, "It had never crossed my mind up until that point that there might be doors closed to me simply because I was a girl."[17] Today, women hold important positions. They are doctors, lawyers, presidents of large companies, astronauts, and almost everything in between. It is easy to forget there was a time when women were not allowed to do many things men did. In the early 1900s, for example, women were not even allowed to vote for the president of the United States. So NASA's reply, though it seemed harsh, was not unusual for the time. But that did not make Hillary any happier to receive it.

The terse response opened Hillary's eyes to what the world was like outside her picture-perfect community of Park Ridge. Church leaders helped her further broaden her understanding. One youth

Hillary Rodham's senior portrait was taken in May 1965 at Maine South High School in Park Ridge, Illinois. Not long after, she would have her liberal awakening at Wellesley College.

minister, Donald Jones, played a particularly large role in that respect. Hillary said Jones "took us to meet black and Hispanic teenagers in downtown Chicago for service and worship exchanges . . . Because my village was so secure, I had a hard time imagining what life was like for those in less fortunate circumstances."[18] In January 1963, Jones took Hillary and a few other students to Chicago's Orchestra Hall to hear a speech by Dr. Martin Luther King Jr. Dr. King was a popular civil rights activist. He believed all people should be treated equally, regardless of the color of their skin. King's speech had a powerful effect on the fifteen-year-old. Hillary later said, "My youth minister from our church took a few of us down on a cold January night to hear someone that we had read about, we had watched on television, we had seen with our own eyes from a distance, this phenomenon known as Dr. King."[19] Seven months later, King led a march on Washington, DC. There he delivered one of the most memorable speeches in history, which became known as his "I have a dream" speech.

As it did many people, King's work inspired Hillary. She continued her political involvement during her high school years. She attended Maine East High School as a freshman, sophomore, and junior. She was a member of her student council and vice president of the junior class. As a senior, she attended Maine South High School. There she ran for student body president against several boys. One opponent told her she was crazy if she thought a girl could be elected president. Hillary lost the election but learned another valuable lesson about what roles the real world felt women should have.

Hillary soon joined a school group called the Young Republicans. In 1964, she campaigned for Republican presidential candidate Barry Goldwater. She and the candidate's other young women supporters were called Goldwater Girls. Goldwater lost the election to Democrat Lyndon B. Johnson. Johnson had once been John F. Kennedy's vice president and had become president when Kennedy was assassinated in 1963. Hillary's candidate may not have won, yet she had learned a lot about the way politics work. Years later, after Goldwater learned Hillary had campaigned for him, he invited her to his home for a visit.[20]

Given her good grades and the expectations of her parents, it was clear Hillary was headed for college. The question was: Which one? Two of her younger high school teachers helped guide her decision. Hillary said, "One had graduated from Wellesley and the other graduated from Smith. They'd been assigned to teach in my high school, and they were so bright and smart and terrific."[21] Hillary was inspired to be like them. She applied to both of the all-female schools, which encouraged women to become involved in politics and world affairs. The active student, ranked near the top of her class, was accepted to both. Her decision on which to attend came down to something simple. Hillary said, "I decided on Wellesley based on the photographs of the campus."[22] A picture, she thought, was worth a thousand words. That was one word for each mile she would have to travel to get to her new school.

CHAPTER THREE

Class President

· ·

W hen Hillary Rodham and her parents arrived in Wellesley, Massachusetts, they found themselves in an environment that was quite familiar in many ways. As an affluent suburb of Boston, Wellesley had much in common with the suburban Chicago milieu of Park Ridge. One can easily imagine a stroll through Wellesley's leafy streets in the autumn chill providing much comfort to the Rodham family. After all, none of the Rodhams had even lived in New England, and now their only daughter would be spending four of her most formative years there.

Located next to Lake Waban, Wellesley College was founded in 1870 with a goal of providing women a liberal, or wide-ranging, education. Those admitted to the school typically were the top students at their high schools, like Hillary. But that did not mean she fit in right away. Like many freshman, she knew no one at the school. The people she did meet seemed far different than those she had known in Park Ridge.

Hillary said, "[Wellesley was] all very rich and fancy and very intimidating to my way of thinking."[1]

One reason Hillary felt that way is because many of the wealthiest families in the United States sent their children to Wellesley. The Rodhams were not poor, but neither were they extraordinarily rich. The trips she had taken to the poor parts of Chicago with her youth minister had introduced her to a lifestyle different from her own. Wellesley introduced her to the lifestyle of the very wealthy.

Day-to-day life at the college was also a lot different from what it had been in the schools Hillary grew up in. The environment at Wellesley was closely controlled. Students had many rules to follow. Their dorms were subject to nightly curfews. Men were allowed in those rooms for only a few hours on Sunday afternoons. When men visited, the dorm room door had to be kept open. Students also had to follow dress codes. At dinner, for example, girls had to wear skirts. The school's history played a role in its formality. Traditionally, Wellesley was known as a

Hillary had trouble adjusting to life at Wellesley at first, but she quickly became comfortable and thrived as a leader in student government and liberal causes.

place where young women went to bide time until they married. Sure, they got a good education when they were there. But, for many parents, making sure their daughters married well was their number one goal. One legend says members of Wellesley's senior class would compete to see who would be the first one to get married after graduation.[2]

Finding Her Place

Wellesley's classes proved to be difficult for Hillary, as well. Everything added up to make her feel like she did not belong. She said, "A month after school started, I called home collect and told my parents I didn't think I was smart enough to be there."[3] Her parents made her stay, and she quickly adjusted. Not having boys on campus helped. When she went to class, she did not worry about her looks, which allowed her to focus on learning. NASA told her she could not become an astronaut. In high school, she was told there was no way a girl could win the position of student body president. But at Wellesley, she could be anything she wanted to be. In time, she did just that.

Hillary was soon elected president of Wellesley's Young Republicans. The selection made a lot of sense, since she had been a member of a similar group in high school. She had also grown up supporting and working for Republicans. But, despite her experience with the party, Hillary soon began wondering if being a Republican was the right choice. She said, "My doubts about the party and its policies were growing, particularly when it came to civil rights and the Vietnam War."[4]

The Antiwar Movement

The Vietnam War began in 1957 as a battle between North Vietnam and South Vietnam. The North was under control of the Communist Party and hoped to take over the non-Communist South. North Vietnam's goal was to overthrow South Vietnam's government and rejoin the two into one Vietnam. The United States was strongly against Communism and did not want this to happen. So, the United States joined the war in the 1960s and sent hundreds of thousands of soldiers to help the South. As the war dragged on, more and more American soldiers were killed.

Back home, Americans were divided on the war. Some believed the United States should be involved. Others believed it should not be. In time, the number of Americans killed in Vietnam grew and support for the war declined. Families were losing their friends and loved ones. Soon, Americans began rallying for the war to end. In 1973, the United States government brought its soldiers home. Estimates say fifty-eight thousand American soldiers were killed in Vietnam, and three hundred thousand were wounded.[5] Two million Vietnamese civilians and soldiers were killed.[6]

Hillary said, "It's hard to explain to young Americans today . . . how obsessed many in my generation were with the Vietnam War . . . The country was divided, leaving us confused about our own feelings. My friends and I constantly discussed and debated it."[7] Although the war ended in 1975, it still evokes strong feelings in people. Many soldiers have never been accounted for.

Soon, Hillary resigned as president of the Young Republicans. She was not only beginning to disagree with the Republican Party, but she was also at odds with President Johnson, a Democrat. Johnson supported the Vietnam War even after many Americans, including Hillary, began to think the country should no longer be involved.

During her junior year at Wellesley, Hillary began campaigning for Democrat Eugene McCarthy. McCarthy was seeking the 1968 Democratic presidential nomination. He was also strongly against the Vietnam War. On weekends, Hillary drove to New Hampshire to help McCarthy's campaign. Many college students who were frustrated with the war did the same. New Hampshire's primary elections were to be the first held in the United States. Doing well in that state would get any presidential candidate off to a good start. Even with the students' help, McCarthy eventually lost the party's nomination to Vice President Hubert Humphrey. But he did fare well in New Hampshire, where Hillary and others had helped. The experience kept Hillary's interest in politics high.

Summer Internship

The summer before her senior year of college, Hillary was chosen to be an intern in Washington, DC. Working in the country's capital city was a great opportunity for her. She was seeking a degree in political science—the study of politics—and Washington, DC, is the center of the country's political machine. Hillary certainly was grateful for the opportunity, but only to a point. She objected when she was assigned to work with Republican members of Congress. But if she wanted to remain in the program she had to work with her former party. She decided to do so and went to work for Republican congressman Harold Collier from her home state of Illinois. When the internship was over, the person in charge of the program had good things to say about Hillary. He said, "She presented her viewpoints very forcibly, always had ideas, always defended what she had in mind."[8]

While in Washington, DC, Hillary and a few others were asked to go to Miami to the Republican National Convention. They were there to help New York governor Nelson Rockefeller win his party's presidential nomination. Rockefeller was not a Democrat, but Hillary went anyway. The candidate eventually lost the Republican nomination to Richard Nixon. Nixon went on to become the thirty-seventh president of the United States.

Turbulent Times

When Hillary's work was done, she returned to her family's home in Park Ridge for the rest of the summer. During that time, she traveled with friend Betsy Johnson into Chicago during the Democratic National Convention. For several reasons, the country was suffering great unrest. Dr. Martin Luther King Jr., whose speech had inspired Hillary five years earlier, had recently been assassinated. She took the news of his death hard. Her college roommate said Hillary entered the room crying and threw her book bag into a wall. Then she shouted, "I can't stand it anymore! I can't take anymore!"[9]

An important senator who was running for president, Robert Kennedy, the former attorney general of the United States and brother of assassinated president John F. Kennedy, had also been recently killed. The Vietnam War still was being fought, and many soldiers were dying.

For those reasons and others, many people were upset with the government. So they decided to protest during the convention. Those protestors and police were fighting everywhere. Riots broke out, and several

Hillary is pictured collaborating with friends during her student days at Wellesley College. She reportedly preferred attending a single sex institution, as it allowed her to focus on her studies and worry less about her appearance.

people were arrested. Hillary said, "Betsy and I were shocked by the police brutality we saw."[10] Her friend was even more explicit. She said, "We saw kids our age getting their heads beaten in. And the police were doing the beating. Hillary and I just looked at each other. We had had a wonderful childhood in Park Ridge, but we obviously hadn't gotten the whole story."[11]

By the time she entered her senior year at Wellesley, Hillary was a full-fledged Democrat. She also had decided to go to law school to become a lawyer. Now, she had to pick a school. Just as she had when choosing a college four years prior, Hillary narrowed her choices to two. This time it was Yale and Harvard. Both colleges were part of the Ivy League, considered to be one of the top groups of schools in the country. Hillary was having a hard time making her final decision. Because it was only a few miles away from Wellesley, Harvard made a lot of sense. That is until Hillary went to a reception at the school. After she was introduced to one of Harvard's professors, her mind was made up. The professor said, "First of all, we have no nearest competitor, and, secondly, we don't need any more women."[12] Not surprisingly, Hillary chose Yale.

Senior Leadership

First, she had to complete her senior year at Wellesley. She was elected president of the Class of 1969. She was very active in this role and even invited Saul Alinsky to speak to the student body. Alinsky was controversial but well known for being a motivational speaker capable of organizing people together to rally for change. Hillary also interviewed Alinsky for her senior thesis, or research project.

As the end of the school year neared, one of Hillary's classmates suggested it would be nice to have a student speak during their graduation ceremony. The problem was it had never been done before. Hillary's friend told the school's president, Ruth Adams, that her class would like to have a speaker. The president initially said no but finally decided to hear more when she was told the students might hold their own ceremony if they did not get their way. As class president, Hillary took it from there. She asked Adams why she was against letting a student speak. She also told her she was the one chosen to speak. A few days before graduation, Adams finally agreed with the students. After nearly one hundred years, Wellesley would have a student speak at graduation. The pressure was on Hillary, who had no idea what she was going to say. She had little time to figure it out. Her classmates proved to be a big help. As she was writing her speech, her friends were sliding notes with their ideas under the door of her dorm room.[14]

Preparing to become the first-ever student graduation speaker was not the only stress Hillary

When she was student body president at Wellesley College in the late 1960s, Hillary Clinton, by her own account, stayed up all night trying to talk other students out of protests against the Vietnam War. [13]

was going through. Her mother was sick back home in Park Ridge and could not travel to see her daughter graduate. Her busy father was not going to attend, either, but when he heard his daughter was going to speak, Hugh Rodham decided to go. Adding to Hillary's stress was the knowledge of who would be speaking before her—United States senator Edward Brooke. Three years earlier, when Hillary was still a Republican, she had campaigned to get Brooke elected. Now, she was going to be speaking on the same stage. The two disagreed on many issues.

Rodham felt let down by the senator's speech. He had not talked about any of the issues she felt her generation was struggling with, such as the Vietnam War and civil rights. "The Senator seemed out of touch with his audience," Rodham later wrote in her autobiography. "His words were aimed at a different Wellesley, one that predated the upheavals of the 1960s."[15]

Dressed in cap and gown and wearing her familiar oversized glasses, Hillary began her speech. First, she talked about issues she believed the senator should have addressed. Her words encouraged students to continue to protest, even though the senator said not to. Her speech argued against many of the ideas Senator Brooke had spoken about minutes earlier. Hillary's speech elicited reactions from nearly all of the two thousand people in the audience. In general, the older people felt uncomfortable and the younger people were inspired. But nobody was unmoved when she said she would like to see a world where people were treated as more than just numbers.

Hillary poses in her graduation cap and gown in 1969. Her commencement address was polarizing. While her classmates tended to share her views, some of the older people in attendance were made uncomfortable by her speech.

When Hillary finished, the front rows of the crowd stood and applauded. Those were her classmates. They cheered their rebellious class president for seven straight minutes.[16] Others were silent, shocked that a twenty-one-year-old woman had spoken such harsh words in front of, and about, a well-known politician. Hillary herself was shocked over the next few days, as the media started to report on how she had upstaged a popular senator.

But what she said had been important—to her classmates, the audience and, soon, to the entire United States. The impact of her words even surprised Hillary. She said, "I had no idea my speech would generate interest far beyond Wellesley. . . When I called home, however, my mother told me that she had been fielding phone calls from reporters and television shows asking me for interviews and appearances."[17] Hillary ended up granting some of those requests. *Life* magazine featured her as one of the voices of her generation. She also appeared on a TV show in Chicago. The speech made the young woman a celebrity. Few knew the speech was not supposed to happen just a few days earlier.

Hillary did not bask in the spotlight for long. After graduation, in fact, she moved far from it. She spent the summer working in Alaska. There, she washed dishes and worked in a fish plant. She was fired from the fish plant when she pointed out that some of the fish looked rotten. Hillary said, "When I told the manager, he fired me and told me to come back the next afternoon to pick up my last check."[18] Hillary said when she showed up the next day, the entire business was gone.

CHAPTER FOUR

Rodham Meets Clinton

· · · · · · · · · · ·

During her four years at Wellesley, Hillary Rodham steadily acclimated to student life out East. Thus, the short move from Wellesley, Massachusetts, to New Haven, Connecticut, where she would attend Yale Law School would not represent culture shock. Yale and Wellesley were both wealthy and venerable institutions with storied histories, but neither was immune to the social upheavals of the 1960s. Political activism and organized student protests were common on most universities campuses by 1969, and the elite schools Hillary attended were no exception.

However, female students were still fairly uncommon. Hillary was one of twenty-seven women accepted to the law school. Two hundred and eight men were accepted. That year, 1969, Yale admitted its first group of female undergraduates. Women in America were becoming empowered. It was just happening slowly.

She may have come from an all-women's college, but Hillary was up for the challenge of competing with the men of Yale. The celebrity status she had achieved from her graduation speech helped boost her confidence.

Starting Off Strong

Hillary continued tackling issues such as civil rights and the Vietnam War during her first year at Yale Law School. Nationally, a couple of key events related to those issues occurred during the year. In April 1970, eight Black Panthers (an African American civil rights group) were put on trial in New Haven. The Black Panthers were accused of murder, but many felt the government had set them up. When the trials took place, thousands of angry people gathered in the city to protest.

Hillary also was deeply affected by what happened in Kent, Ohio, that May. Hundreds of demonstrators gathered at Kent State University to protest President Nixon's announcement that the United States was expanding the Vietnam War into the country of Cambodia. The Kent State protests quickly grew out of hand. Some demonstrators set fires, threw bottles, and cursed at police. The governor called in the National Guard to regain order, but it did not help much. On May 4, members of the National Guard shot and killed four students and injured several others.

Hillary cried over the situation. She said, "I remember rushing out the door of the law school in tears."[1] Hillary had always advocated the right to protest, but she also believed those protests should be peaceful. She never wanted them to end as they had at Kent State University.

Hillary Rodham believed deeply in the mission of the Children's Defense Fund (CDF), founded by activist writer Marian Wright Edelman, above. Hillary accepted an unpaid position with the CDF during law school.

• •

Hillary did not have long to focus on the negative. Three days after the shootings, she spoke at a League of Women Voters meeting in Washington, DC. She made an important connection there. The main speaker was a woman named Marian Wright Edelman. Edelman was a graduate of Yale Law School and an activist. She had started a group that would later become the Children's Defense Fund. She offered Hillary a summer job but did not have money to pay her. Hillary felt strongly about what Edelman was trying to accomplish, so she got a grant to pay for her to live in Washington, DC, and took the job. Edelman's work had a huge impact on the college student. Hillary said,

"I knew right away that I had to go to work for her."[2] In part, the job involved researching the lives of poor children. The experience of working with children had an impact on Hillary. So much so, in fact, that when she returned to Yale, she decided to focus her studies on children's rights.

Law School Romance

Shortly into her second year in law school, another matter captured Hillary's attention. This time, it was a handsome law student from Arkansas. His name was Bill Clinton. There was an obvious attraction between the two from the beginning. Both later said they had seen each other around campus a few times and each had found the other attractive. But for a long time they did not talk to each other. That is, until one day in the library.

After catching Bill staring at her, Hillary decided to break the ice. She said, "If you're going to keep staring at me and I'm going to keep staring back, we ought to at least know each other's names. Mine's Hillary Rodham. What's yours?"[3] The two talked for a short time, and then Hillary left. A few days later, they ran into each other again. Hillary was on her way to register for classes. Bill said that was where he was going, too. In reality, he had already registered. He just wanted to spend time with Hillary. When the two got to the front of the line, the worker said, "Bill, what are you doing back here? You registered this morning."[4] Bill was caught. Hillary laughed at her crush's lie. Soon, they were dating. Hillary and Bill were from different backgrounds. Hillary had grown up comfortably in what was considered a traditional American family. Bill was born in the poor city of Hope, Arkansas, as William Jefferson Blythe III. Bill's father died in an accident three months before his son was born on August 19, 1946. Four years later, the young boy's mother married a car salesman named Roger Clinton. Roger Clinton officially adopted Bill when he was in his teens. It was a nice gesture, but the family's lives still were nowhere near perfect. Bill Clinton described his stepfather as abusive and violent, especially when he drank alcohol. Bill's mother would often remove him and his younger brother from the house to protect them. In a book he wrote years later, Bill Clinton described one terrifying fight between his mother and stepfather. He said, "They were screaming at each other in their bedroom ... I walked out into the hall to the doorway of the bedroom. Just as I did [Roger Clinton] pulled a gun from behind his back and fired in Mother's direction."[5] The bullet landed in the wall between mother and child. The police were called and Roger Clinton was taken to jail. The couple eventually divorced. Later, Bill Clinton's mother remarried.

Through his tumultuous childhood, Bill Clinton somehow remained a good student. By the time he met Hillary, he had graduated from Georgetown University in Washington, DC. He also had won a prestigious Rhodes Scholarship, which took him to England to study. Though they came from different backgrounds, both Bill and Hillary were well educated.

Both students also had a strong interest in politics. Bill had known since he was a teenager that he wanted to serve the public. Hillary had also been involved with politics since she was young. The couple soon became inseparable and moved into an apartment together before Hillary's third year at Yale. In the summer of 1972, they moved together to Texas to work to get George McGovern, a Democratic senator from South Dakota, elected president. McGovern lost the race, but both Hillary and Bill made some important political connections during his campaign.

The meeting of Bill Clinton and Hillary Clinton at Yale Law School sparked a partnership that would prove to be an important part of US history.

Students typically graduate from law school in three years. Hillary decided to postpone her law degree for a year to study child development. So, her final year at Yale was mainly spent working on issues close to her heart. She did research at the Yale Child Study Center and worked with foster families at the New Haven Legal Services office. She even helped write a book. The extra year in school also allowed her to spend more time with Bill. Hillary and Bill graduated from Yale Law School in the spring of 1973. They then flew to England to visit many of the places Bill had seen during his time studying there. At the end of the trip, they stopped at Lake District National Park. There, on the shores of a glacier-fed lake named Ennerdale, Bill asked Hillary to marry him.

Hillary had known the question would someday come. She also had known there would not be an easy answer because both had ambitious career goals. She planned to be a big-city lawyer in someplace like New York City or Washington, DC. Bill planned to go back to his home state of Arkansas to become a politician. Bill's question forced Hillary to make an important life decision. Would she choose her career or love? Hillary said, "I was desperately in love with him but utterly confused about my life and future. So I said, 'No, not now.' What I meant was, 'Give me time.'"[6]

When the couple returned to the United States, they took a brief trip to Arkansas so Hillary could visit the state where Bill had grown up and where he would soon be living again. He had accepted a job to teach at the University of Arkansas Law School in Fayetteville. There, he would plan the political career he had talked about since he was a teen. When summer ended, the pair moved apart.

High-Profile Work

Hillary moved back to Massachusetts to begin her plan of working with children. Marian Wright Edelman, whom Hillary had worked for in the summer of 1970, hired her as an attorney for the Children's Defense Fund. The job required a lot of traveling. On the road, Hillary sometimes visited children in deplorable conditions. She said, "I found children who weren't in school because of physical disabilities like blindness and deafness . . . I met a girl in a wheelchair, who told me how much she wanted to go to school. She knew she couldn't go because she couldn't walk."[7] The experience broke her heart, but Hillary still loved her job because she believed she was making a difference.

Hillary's other passion was fifteen hundred miles away. Bill Clinton had decided to give politics a try sooner than most expected. He announced a run for the US House of Representatives. It was obvious he was planning to stay in Arkansas. If Hillary wanted to be with him, she would have to move. She strongly considered it. She had passed the Arkansas bar exam, so she would be allowed to practice law in that state. It appeared love was going to win out over her big-city aspirations. But a phone call in January 1974 stopped her from moving.

The House Judiciary Committee, a branch of the House of Representatives, had recently selected attorney John Doar to lead the impeachment proceedings against President Nixon. If Nixon were impeached, he would be removed from office. The Republican president had been accused of hiring burglars to spy on Democrats, then trying to cover it up. The scandal was called Watergate, after the Washington building where the crimes had taken place. Watergate was most famously known as a hotel but also housed many offices, including the offices of the Democratic National Committee that were broken into.

Doar needed a team of lawyers to assist him with the impeachment process. He called Bill Clinton to ask if he wanted to help. Bill was not interested in moving to Washington, DC, for the job. Doar called the next person on his list: Hillary Rodham. The opportunity to work on a case against a United States president was too good for Hillary to refuse. She took the job

> "I knew I was happier with Bill than without him."

and moved to Washington. There, she worked with a team of forty-four lawyers. The hours were long, and the team worked seven days a week to build a case against President Nixon. When a tape recording of the president rehearsing lies about the break-in was released in August 1974, Hillary's job was all but over. That evidence was so strong, the president knew he would most likely be convicted of the crimes he was charged with. So, on August 9, 1974, Nixon resigned from office.

Nixon's resignation officially ended Hillary's job. She had no idea what she was going to do next. She decided to act on an earlier offer to teach law at the

University of Arkansas. Finally, she and Bill could be together again. Hillary said, "I knew I was happier with Bill than without him."[8]

On to Arkansas

Many people did not want Hillary to move to Fayetteville. Because Arkansas was generally considered a poor state located in the middle of "nowhere," Hillary's friends thought she was crazy to go there. She could work anywhere in the country, so why there? Bill's family, especially his mother, Virginia, also did not want Hillary to move to Fayetteville. His mother thought Hillary was too plain and did not care enough about appearances. Virginia spent a lot of time on her own looks and expected other women to do the same. For that reason and others, she felt Hillary was not good enough for her son. Some of Bill's congressional campaign staff members also did not like the idea of having Hillary around. They thought she would be a distraction and hurt his chances of getting elected.

Stubborn and in love, Hillary went anyway. She moved into her own house and began teaching at the university. She also helped Bill's campaign. In November, Bill lost a close election. Afterward, he resumed his teaching job.

In the summer of 1975, Bill drove Hillary to the airport so she could visit friends in Chicago and on the East Coast. On the way, the couple passed a small brick house with a "For Sale" sign in the front yard. As they drove past, Hillary mentioned how much she liked the place, which was priced at $20,500. When she returned from her trip, Bill picked her up at the airport. He asked

In 1975, Bill Clinton purchased a special property in Fayetteville, Arkansas. Legend has it that he used the new home to persuade Hillary to marry him. Indeed, the two were married there later that year. It is now known as the Clinton House Museum.

• •

if she remembered the house. Then he said, "I bought it. You have to marry me now, because I can't live there alone."[9] After two years of being asked and answering that she was not ready, Hillary finally said yes.

Their engagement was short. The couple married in the small house's living room on October 11, 1975. Two months later, they honeymooned in Acapulco, Mexico, with Hillary's two brothers and parents along. Though most women took the last name of their husband after marriage, Hillary decided to keep her own name. "I need to maintain my interests and my commitments. I need my own identity, too," she said.[10]

Back home in Arkansas, the newlyweds resumed their teaching jobs. But Bill was nowhere near ready to give up politics. In May 1976, he decided to run for attorney general of Arkansas. The attorney general is the head law officer and legal adviser to the government. In November, Bill was elected to the position. He and Hillary sold their little house and moved to the state capital of Little Rock.

Moving meant Hillary had to give up her job at the university. She decided to go into private practice and was hired by the Rose Law Firm. One of the firm's partners was a man named Vince Foster. Hillary had met Foster while teaching at the University of Arkansas. She continued working for children's rights with the firm and went to trial in several cases. As had happened many other times, the pressure was on Hillary at her new job. She was the first female lawyer the highly respected law firm had ever hired. She was also the main breadwinner for her family. Bill may have been in a powerful government position, but the job did not pay well. Hillary had to pay for many of their expenses.

Being the wife of a well-known public official brought Hillary a lot of attention. She said, "Wives of elected officials were constantly scrutinized."[11] The unwanted attention reaffirmed what her mother-in-law had told her: appearances were important to people in the South. That was good for Bill. His charm, wit, and boyish good looks had made him a popular attorney general and helped him get elected. He was so popular, in fact, that he decided to run for governor. After winning the Democratic nomination, he went on to be elected

45

to the position. At age thirty-two, he was the youngest governor in the United States.

The following year, Hillary became a partner, or equal, at her law firm in Arkansas. The president of the United States, Jimmy Carter, had even appointed her to the board of a corporation that gave legal assistance to the poor. Hillary and her new husband had achieved a lot in the five years since they had graduated from law school. As young as they were, more success was certain to come. What they did not know was that there would be many tough times as well.

CHAPTER FIVE

Governor's Mansion

• •

The tail end of the 1970s was a momentous time for the couple. Bill Clinton was sworn in as governor of Arkansas in January 1979. Their daughter, Chelsea Victoria Clinton, was born February 27, 1980, a little over a year later. With Bill's gubernatorial victory, Hillary's advancing legal career, and now the birth of a healthy baby girl, the couple was achieving many of their major life goals together.

Hillary had no intention of quitting her job as a lawyer to be a full-time First Lady and mother. Yet she did take four months off work to stay home with her new daughter. Her bonding experience with Chelsea led her to believe even more strongly that working women should be allowed to have some paid time off after giving birth. She was fortunate enough to be able to do that. She knew many women could not.

Keeping her job turned out to be a wise move. In 1980, Bill Clinton lost his re-election bid. So, in the beginning of 1981, the family moved out of the Governor's Mansion.

They bought a house in Little Rock, and Bill took a job with a local law firm.

New Name, New Style

Over the years, the pressure on Hillary from family and the general public to change her last name continued to grow. When Hillary's mother sent letters to the couple, she addressed them to "Mr. and Mrs. Bill Clinton."[1] Bill's mother felt so strongly about the issue that she had cried when she was told Hillary was not changing her name.[2] Equally important was the reaction from the general public. A lot of people felt it was odd for a woman to keep her maiden name after marriage. It was not at all common at the time. When Bill decided to again run for governor in 1982, Hillary made her own big decision. Despite believing a name should not matter, she decided to change hers. Hillary Rodham became Hillary Clinton. She said, "It was not a decision that was easy to make for me, but it was one that I made, thinking it was the best for me and the best for my husband."[3] She wanted the criticism to end.

Hillary Clinton also changed her appearance. She replaced her big-framed glasses with contact lenses. She began wearing more fashionable clothes. She even updated her hairstyle. How much it all helped is unknown, but, with a lot of campaign assistance from his wife, Bill Clinton won the election. The family moved out of their private home and back into the Governor's Mansion. The help Hillary gave her husband to become governor also helped her. Bill selected Hillary to head the Arkansas Education Standards Committee. The group's

As First Lady of Arkansas, Hillary Clinton successfully tackled education reform. This was her first high-profile political initiative. Here, she appears at a conference for educational standards in Little Rock in 1983.

main focus was on the quality of education across the state. Big changes were needed in that area because Arkansas residents were among the poorest and least educated in America. Given Hillary's experience with educational issues, the job was perfect. With her help, important legislation to reform Arkansas schools passed the legislature. For that and other reasons, a newspaper chose Hillary Clinton as its Arkansas Woman of the Year in 1984.

The Clintons Gain Political Momentum

Bill Clinton kept getting reelected and remained governor of Arkansas until 1992, a total of twelve years. His popularity was extremely high during that time. He was so well liked, in fact, that many encouraged him to run for president in 1988. He considered it but decided not to. Republican George H. W. Bush won that year's election to become the forty-first president of the United States.

The Clintons remained in Arkansas and continued to help that state grow. Hillary Clinton achieved many great things as First Lady. She brought a program called HIPPY (Home Instruction Program for Preschool Youngsters) to the state. The program helped get young preschool-aged children ready to enter the school system. Hillary also remained involved with the Children's Defense Fund.

In many ways, life as a Clinton appeared to be perfect. Those appearances were deceiving. During his years in office, Bill Clinton had gained a reputation as a womanizer, a man who has an interest in many women. Rumors were everywhere. The most notorious relationship he had was with a woman named Gennifer Flowers. Flowers met Bill Clinton in 1977, when she was working as a television reporter. She later claimed she had an affair with him for more than ten years. Bill denied it for a long time. Years later, he admitted he had an affair with Flowers. Some say Hillary knew her husband was seeing other women and chose to ignore it. Others think she did not know. Hillary has addressed the issue several times. She once said, "I don't talk about it. I think my marriage is my marriage and my relationship with my husband is solely between us."[4]

> **I think my marriage is my marriage and my relationship with my husband is solely between us.**

If people knew about Bill Clinton's alleged womanizing, they did not seem to care much. He remained a popular governor. Meanwhile, President Bush grew unpopular with many citizens. Pressure on Bill to run for the country's highest office again grew. Chelsea's age was one of the reasons he had decided not to run in 1988. His daughter was only seven at that time and being president is a time-consuming duty. Bill said he did not want to be away from his daughter as much as he would be if he were president. But Chelsea was eleven when the next election cycle came around, and the Clintons had spent a lot of time getting her ready for the amount of negative attention their family would receive during a presidential race. To prepare, one parent would pretend to say bad things

51

Arkansas governor Bill Clinton announces his intention to run for president. By his side at this 1991 press conference are wife Hillary and daughter Chelsea. The presidency would challenge the couple personally and politically like nothing that came before.

• •

about the other to teach Chelsea how to react. Hillary told her daughter, "By the time this is over, they'll attack you, they'll attack your cat, they'll attack your goldfish."[5]

Chelsea said she could handle the pressure and encouraged her father to run for president. In September 1991, Bill Clinton made up his mind: he would enter the presidential race. The announcement speech he made on October 3 in Little Rock made it official. He said, "Today I am declaring my candidacy for President of the United States. Together I believe we can provide leadership that will restore the American dream—that will fight for the forgotten middle class—that will provide more opportunity, insist on more responsibility and create a greater sense of community for this great country."[6] His inspirational message of hope was similar to what Hillary had said years ago in her college graduation speech. Bill hoped it would be as successful as his wife's had been.

Some in Arkansas were upset by Bill Clinton's announcement. They had voted him governor because he promised he would complete his term in that office. If elected president, he could not do that. But Bill felt he could spread his mission to a wider audience as president. Besides, running for president is not an opportunity many get. Others in Arkansas were supportive and happy to see someone from their state run for president. Bill also had a powerful and successful team member built in. Hillary said, "If you vote for my husband, you get me; it's a two-for-one, blueplate special."[7] Many believed Hillary was helping her husband so much behind the scenes they were basically one person. Soon, the nickname of "Billary" was used to describe the two.

CHAPTER SIX

Road to Washington

· · · · · · · · · · · · · · · · · · ·

B ill Clinton was a long shot for the Democratic presidential nomination. Despite multiple accusations of philandering, Clinton was nonetheless an extremely popular figure as the governor of Arkansas. This popularity did not necessarily translate to the national stage, however. In fact, his biggest national audience was at the 1988 Democratic National Convention, when he gave a speech in support of Michael Dukakis's unsuccessful candidacy against George H. W. Bush. Many observers felt the speech was too long, which Hillary acknowledged as detrimental to her husband's political career. Four years later, he would receive the nomination for the nation's highest office and prove his critics wrong.

The allegations of Bill Clinton's womanizing followed him into his candidacy. Gennifer Flowers had tape-recorded some conversations she had with him. The recordings made Bill appear guilty of having an affair with her. When the Flowers tapes were released, many thought Clinton's chances of becoming president were over. But Hillary felt her husband had done nothing wrong. She believed someone, most likely the Republican Party, was trying to ruin Bill's chances of becoming president by paying Flowers to say what she said. Hillary said of Flowers's story, "It's not true. I just don't believe any of that. All of these people, including that woman, have denied this many, many times. I'm not going to speculate on her motive. We know she was paid."[1]

People wanted answers. If he was innocent, why would he, a married man, spend so much time talking to another woman on the telephone? Hillary Clinton had an explanation. She said, "Anybody who knows my husband knows that he bends over backwards to help people who are in trouble and is always willing to listen to their problems."[2]

> "I'm not sitting here—some little woman standing by her man like Tammy Wynette. I'm sitting here because I love him, and I honor what we've been through together."

Stand by Your Man

If they wanted to save Bill's chances of becoming president, the Clintons had to act out against the negative publicity. In January 1992, they went on a national television program to talk about the Flowers situation. Their interview was shown immediately after the Super Bowl, one of the most-watched programs of the year. The interviewer asked Bill Clinton if he had had an affair with Flowers. Clinton said, "The allegation is false."[3] When the interviewer referred to the couple's marriage as an "arrangement," Hillary became visibly upset. She said, "I'm not sitting here—some little woman standing by her man like Tammy Wynette. I'm sitting here because I love him, and I honor what we've been through together . . . If that's not enough for people, then heck, don't vote for him."[4]

Hillary's reference to Tammy Wynette upset the famous country singer and many of her fans. Wynette demanded an apology. By "standing by her man,"

Steve Kroft interviewed the Clintons for the CBS television show ***60 Minutes*** **in 1992. Hillary's response to questions about Bill's alleged infidelity rankled many Americans.**

Hillary was referring to a song Wynette had written in the 1960s called "Stand by Your Man." The woman in the song stood by her man when he did something she did not "understand," but Wynette herself was a strong woman. She found Hillary Clinton's comment insulting. Hillary later apologized. She said, "I didn't mean to hurt Tammy Wynette as a person. I happen to be a country-western fan. If she feels like I've hurt her feelings, I'm sorry about that."[5] The controversy was another hard lesson for the Clintons. They had been in the public eye much of their lives, but the scrutiny the Clintons received when Bill became a presidential

Early in 1992, Bill and Hillary were in the home stretch of a presidential campaign. Despite some public-relations hiccups, Hillary was a tremendous asset to her husband's campaign.

candidate was greater than they ever had experienced. Even when Hillary did something as simple as change her hairstyle, it became a story somewhere.

Embattled Reputations

In February 1992, the *Wall Street Journal* ran an article that angered many people. It claimed Bill Clinton had dodged the draft during the Vietnam War. Many Americans have strong beliefs that those called upon should serve their country if they are selected. These people were upset with the allegation that Bill had dodged the draft. His reputation suffered because of it.

Amazingly, not only did Bill Clinton remained in the presidential race, but he won the Democratic Party's nomination for the 1992 presidential election.

A Winning Strategy

There was little time to rest or celebrate. Of the three main presidential candidates, Bill Clinton was third in the polls. The current president, Republican George H. W. Bush, was running again and was more popular than Clinton. Another man, Ross Perot, was running as an independent and was more popular, too.

First, Clinton chose a United States senator from Tennessee, Al Gore, as his running mate. Gore would become vice president if Clinton were elected president. Gore was similar to Bill Clinton in many ways. Hillary Clinton and Gore's wife, Tipper, also had a lot in common. Both were accomplished, independent, opinionated, and powerful women.

During long bus rides on the campaign trail, the Clintons quickly bonded with vice presidential pick Al Gore and his wife, Tipper. Crowds responded to the youth and vitality of the two couples.

• • • • • • • • • • • • • • • • • • • •

In July, the Clintons and Gores began touring across the United States in a bus. Hillary named the tour "Bill, Al, Hillary and Tipper's Excellent Adventures,"[6] after a popular movie of the time. The candidates and their wives traveled the country and talked to voters along the way. The two couples hardly knew each other when they began but grew close to each other on the trip.

In addition to the bus campaign, the Clintons flew to several states to speak to voters. In November, the hard work paid off. Bill Clinton defeated both President Bush and Perot in the election. Clinton received 43 percent of the popular, or citizen, vote. Less than half of Americans had chosen him on their ballots. Many critics held this fact against Clinton throughout the course of his presidency.

When President Bush called to concede the 1992 race, Hillary said, "I was overwhelmed . . . Bill and I went into our bedroom, closed the door and prayed together for God's help as he took on this awesome honor and responsibility."[7]

Bill Clinton was about to become the forty-second president of the United States. He was only forty-six years old. He had been a young governor. Now, he was going to be a young president. Hillary would be the country's First Lady. Many wondered exactly what she would do in that position. She did, too. She said, "I had to decide what I wanted to do with the opportunities and responsibilities I had inherited."[8] As she usually did, Hillary made the most of those opportunities.

CHAPTER SEVEN

First Couple

· · · · · · · · · · · · · · · · · · · ·

On January 20, 1993, Hillary Rodham Clinton stood beside her husband as he was sworn in as the forty-second president of the United States. The inauguration was well attended, despite the cold and damp winter weather in Washington, D.C. Maya Angelou read a poem called "On the Pulse of Morning," signifying a rebirth of optimism for the nation. President Clinton's inaugural speech echoed this sentiment while also presaging the globalist agenda that would become one of the hallmarks of his presidency: "To renew America, we must meet challenges abroad as well as at home. There is no longer a clear division between what is foreign and what is domestic. The world economy, the world environment...they affect us all. Today, as an older order passes, the new world is more free but less stable."[1]

The family's belongings had been shipped from Arkansas to the White House immediately after Bill Clinton was sworn into office. Hillary was no stranger

Hillary Clinton and daughter Chelsea look on as Chief Justice William Rehnquist swears in William Jefferson Clinton as the forty-second president of the United States.

• •

to the massive building she was about to call home. She had been inside before. But she still was overwhelmed by her new home and life. She said, "It was during my walk up the path toward the White House ... that the reality hit me: I was actually the First Lady, married to the President of the United States."[2]

> It was during my walk up the path toward the White House ... that the reality hit me: I was actually the First Lady, married to the President of the United States.

1600 Pennsylvania Avenue

The White House, located at 1600 Pennsylvania Avenue in Washington, DC, is one of the best-known buildings in the United States. The country's first president, George Washington, ordered construction to begin in 1792. Sadly, the building was not completed during Washington's lifetime. The first presidential couple to live there was John Adams and his wife, Abigail. They began living there in 1800. The presidential mansion was not called the White House until one hundred years later. The inside of the building is 55,000 square feet (5,110 sq km), roughly the size of an entire city block. There are 132 rooms, 35 bathrooms, 28 fireplaces, a running track, a movie theater, a bowling lane, and a swimming pool. The White House kitchen has five full-time chefs.[3]

New Role for the First Lady

Once the celebrations died down, the Clintons went to work. When Bill was governor of Arkansas, he had appointed his wife to a job leading an important education committee. This time, laws would not allow him to appoint her to a high-level position. It is not as if she needed something to keep her busy. For Hillary, being the First Lady was a full-time job. It was her decision for it to be that way.

Throughout history, First Ladies have played a variety of roles. Hillary's time as First Lady promised to be different than many of those who preceded her. She was not a traditional homemaker. She was not particularly glamorous. Throughout her husband's political career, she had played a vital role in his political decisions. The couple had become known as "Billary" for a reason. The dozens of women who served as First Lady before Hillary all had been important. But few had been as independent and as strong-willed as Hillary Clinton.

Hillary began her job as First Lady with a staff of twenty workers. There were specific duties she was supposed to attend to. The area of the White House where she and her staff worked soon became known as "Hillaryland." Her group's main purpose was to help support the president's agenda, especially with issues related to women, children, and families.[4] All were areas Hillary was familiar with and passionate about.

In the first month of his presidency, Bill Clinton found an official position for his wife when he formed a task force to discuss health care reform. The task force's goal was to make sure every American could afford to be treated for medical problems. President Clinton promised that would be done in one hundred days. The plan was criticized for several reasons. Most thought the deadline was far too short. How could he accomplish in a little more than three months something others had not been able to do in years? But with his wife leading the battle, the president was confident. Hillary was not paid for her work, but the decision to pick her was criticized anyway. One group even unsuccessfully sued the task force. The group said it was illegal for the president's wife to be in charge. In the end, the task force did not meet its

As First Lady, one of Hillary Clinton's early challenges was to tackle health care reform. On September 28, 1993, she testified before the House Ways and Means Committee, pledging to improve health care for all.

• •

hundred-day deadline. Hillary said, "I have never seen an issue that is as complicated as this. I can see why for fifty years people have tiptoed toward this problem and turned around and ran away."[5]

In the midst of it all, Hillary's father had a stroke. Hillary and Chelsea flew to Arkansas, where Hugh and Dorothy Rodham had moved, to be with him in the hospital. Soon after, Hugh Rodham died. His sad daughter wrote, "I couldn't help but think how my relationship with my father had evolved over time. I adored him as a little girl . . . but I was overwhelmed with sadness for what he would now be missing . . . I was thankful for the life, opportunities and dreams he passed along to me."[6]

Losing her father was tough on Hillary. And more stress was on its way. The Clintons were about to be confronted by some major distractions that would threaten Bill Clinton's presidency and place the couple's marriage in jeopardy.

Travelgate and Whitewater Scandals

The first of several big controversies of Bill Clinton's presidency occurred in the spring of 1993. It began when he fired the staff of the White House Travel Office after problems were discovered with the office's financial records. Hillary said she had issues with the way the office was being run. She said, "There was petty cash left lying around. Cash ended up in the personal account of one of the workers . . . that money belongs to people and it should be handled appropriately if it is in any way connected with the White House."[7]

The situation was no big deal until it was revealed that Bill Clinton's cousin was placed in charge of the travel office. Then, many thought the firings were done so a relative of the president could be put in charge. Hillary was accused of being the one who said the staff should be fired. The media came up with a name for the scandal: "Travelgate." After an investigation, the Clintons were found to have done nothing illegal. However, many still believe Hillary demanded the firings. Hillary downplayed her involvement. She said, "I expressed my concern ... that if there were fiscal mismanagement in the Travel Office ... it should be addressed promptly."[8]

Another controversy the Clintons were involved with was called Whitewater. That issue's long story began in the 1970s, when the Clintons and a friend bought some land in Arkansas. Their plan was to divide the property and sell each piece to make money. Years later, the business partner got into legal trouble and the Clintons were also investigated. Some believed illegal money was used to help get people, including Bill Clinton, elected to political office. Several people were convicted of crimes following the investigation. Hillary became the first wife of a president to have to testify before a grand jury. She said, "We didn't do anything wrong. We never intended to do anything wrong."[9] Eventually, the Clintons were cleared of any wrongdoings.

Vince Foster, whom Hillary had worked with at the Rose Law Firm in Arkansas, died while the Whitewater investigation was under way. By that point, Foster was working for the president. Foster's death was ruled a suicide, but because he was connected to the Clintons and involved in many of their controversial dealings, rumors circulated that Foster was murdered in a cover-up. The Clintons deny anything of the sort happened. The Whitewater issue, and Foster's untimely death, plagued the Clintons for years.

The second year of Bill Clinton's presidency did not begin well, either. First, his mother died in January. Then, in May, a woman named Paula Jones, a former employee of the state of Arkansas, sued the president for sexual harassment.

The president was not only having personal problems. He was also having political problems. His party had lost the majority in Congress in the 1994 midterm elections, removing a lot of power from Clinton's presidency.

Meanwhile, Hillary was spending a lot of time defending herself and her husband. She also spent some of her time in 1995 and 1996 writing a book. It was called *It Takes a Village and Other Lessons Children Teach Us.* The book's subject was one that had been important to her for a long time: raising children properly. She said, "What I would hope would come from this book is really a national discussion about what we [parents and society in general] can do better."[10] She accomplished that goal. When it was released in 1996, *It Takes a Village* sold extremely well. Hillary set off on a cross-country tour, where she met with and signed books for thousands of people. The audio version of the book even won a Grammy Award for Best Spoken Word Album in 1997. During that time period, Hillary also helped secure funding for cancer research.

A Second Term

Though the controversial aspects of Clinton's presidency had dominated the news, there were many positives that took place during his first term. He signed a popular bill that allowed workers to take paid time off to care for a sick family member. He signed a bill that required people to wait five days before being able to buy a handgun. The president also adopted a policy that allowed some gays and lesbians to serve in the armed forces. The policy was called "Don't ask, don't tell."

For those and other reasons, Bill Clinton remained a popular president with the American people. In this way, his presidency was similar to his governorship. People had issues with the way he handled his personal life, but they loved the way he did his job. In the 1996 election, Clinton easily defeated both Republican Bob Dole and Independent Ross Perot. Again, he did not receive a majority of the popular vote. Only 49 percent of Americans voted for him. But it did not matter. Bill Clinton would be president of the United States for another four years.

Shortly after Clinton began his second term as president, the White House had one less person living in it. In the fall of 1997, seventeen-year-old Chelsea left for college. She had chosen to attend Stanford University in Northern California. Having her daughter move nearly 3,000 miles (4,828 km) away was tough on Hillary.

By this time, Hillary's role as First Lady had changed. She continued to work on health care issues and her longtime passion of children's issues. But she was no longer her husband's main health care reform adviser. Instead, she took on several other tasks. She became a spokesperson for the United States by traveling to other countries. On trips to Africa, Asia, Europe, Latin America, and more, she spoke out for human rights, health care, and education. In addition to that work, she also played the more-traditional First Lady roles. That meant entertaining guests at the White House for dinners, parties, and other get-togethers.

The Monica Lewinsky Scandal

As the controversy over the Whitewater scandal finally faded from the Clintons' lives, another emerged.

The head of the Whitewater investigation, Kenneth Starr, announced he had discovered the president lied while giving testimony during the Paula Jones sexual harassment case. When he was asked, the president had said he did not have an affair with a White House intern named Monica Lewinsky. Starr believed President Clinton had. He also believed the president had asked Lewinsky to deny the affair if she was asked. If Starr's arguments proved true, President Clinton would be in deep trouble. Lying and asking someone else to lie could lead to impeachment and potential removal from office.

> "We used to say in the White House that if a place is too dangerous, too small or too poor, send the First Lady. [11]

First, though, he would need to be proven guilty of these crimes.

When Hillary Clinton heard about the accusations, she did not believe they were true. Bill Clinton told her he had talked to Lewinsky a few times. He said he had helped her try to find a job. Hillary believed her husband. They had been through plenty of scandals in their lifetimes, some similar to this one. She had no reason to believe this time was any different. She thought it was just another story made up by people who were out to get her husband.

As with most everything concerning the Clintons— especially controversial issues—the media reported the story nonstop. When asked by reporters what she thought about the accusations, Hillary said,

"Certainly I believe they are false. Absolutely."[12] For his part, Bill Clinton stuck to his story. In January 1998, he addressed the country on national television. The angry president said, "I want to say one thing to the American people. I want you to listen to me. I'm going to say this again. I did not have sexual relations with that woman, Miss Lewinsky."[13] Shaking his finger at the camera, the president continued, "I never told anybody to lie, not a single time—never. These allegations are false and I need to go back to work for the American people."[14]

Bill Clinton's story changed a few months later. On August 15, he woke Hillary and told her it had all been true. He did have an affair with Lewinsky. Hillary was stunned. She said, "What do you mean? What are you saying? Why did you lie to me?"[15] Hillary said her husband cried when she told him he had to tell Chelsea. Bill also had lied to his daughter when he told her the affair did not happen.[16]

Two days later, the president gave testimony to a grand jury. Later that night, he went back on national television. This time, he admitted to having an affair with Lewinsky. The president said, "Indeed, I did have a relationship with Miss Lewinsky that was not appropriate. In fact, it was wrong."[17] He said he never asked anyone to lie. Again, he asked the country to stop prying into his private life and let him move on with the important issues.

It was not necessarily guilt that made President Clinton confess. Three weeks before his televised speech, Lewinsky had given attorneys a key piece of physical evidence. The evidence offered proof the affair took place. Many believe the president had learned about the evidence and would never have admitted to the affair if he knew he would not have been caught.

Public opinion was divided on how Hillary Clinton handled herself after finding out her husband had cheated on her and lied, especially after she decided not to get a divorce. Many said she was not holding true to what she said she believed in. She had been so outspoken over the years on women's rights and issues. But many thought that instead of the strong, empowered woman she had always been, she was being weak by allowing her husband to get away with his actions. Others thought she was showing real dedication and doing the right thing by standing by her husband through thick and thin. Still others, like Hillary herself, thought what happened between a husband and wife was a personal matter. Deciding whether or not to stay with her husband was not an easy decision for her to make. She sought the advice of many others and spent weeks thinking about it. Eventually, she chose to stay with her husband and work on the problems they were having with their marriage.

Opinion on how Bill Clinton should be punished for lying was split along party lines. Republicans thought he should be impeached. Democrats thought he should be reprimanded but not impeached. A majority of Americans agreed with the Democrats. On December 19, 1998, the verdict finally came. The

House of Representatives impeached the president for perjury, or telling a lie under oath, and obstruction of justice. Bill Clinton joined Andrew Johnson as the only presidents ever to be impeached. Johnson was impeached in 1868 for removing a member of his cabinet. That was a violation of a controversial law. The United States Supreme Court later declared the law unconstitutional.

Impeachment was only the first step to removing Clinton from office. The Senate still had to vote to remove him. A trial was held to determine whether or not to do so. In February 1999, after twenty-one days of

Not long after leaving the White House and her position as First Lady, Hillary Clinton campaigned for a seat in the US Senate. Her victory allowed her to step outside the shadow of her husband.

debate, the Senate found Bill Clinton not guilty. He was impeached but could remain president.

A Different Race

As her husband's tumultuous final term as president wound down, Hillary Clinton began gearing up for a race of her own. After months of consideration and encouraging pressure from fellow Democrats, Hillary announced she would move to New York and run for a seat in the United States Senate. In doing so, she became the first former First Lady to run for political office. The Clintons bought a house in Chappaqua, New York. After moving, Hillary began her campaign and won her party's nomination for the seat.

Hillary's race, like much of the Clintons' lives, was filled with difficulties. Her Republican opponent was a congressman named Rick Lazio. All along, most people thought her opponent would be Rudy Giuliani, the popular mayor of New York City. But health problems and personal issues prevented Giuliani from running, so Lazio stepped in. The Republican candidate attacked Clinton, saying she did not know anything about New York State or its citizens. Lazio said she only moved there to enter the Senate race.

One of the most controversial moments of the senate campaign had nothing to do with politics. It came when the New York Yankees visited the White House to honor their World Series victory. The team's manager gave Hillary a Yankees cap and she put it on. Since her youthful days as a tomboy in Illinois, Clinton had been a Chicago Cubs fan. Now, she was wearing a New York

Yankees cap. Many took that as a sign that Clinton was willing to do whatever it took to get elected, even if it meant pretending to like something she did not. Hillary had her own explanation for wearing the cap. She told an interviewer, "I am a Cubs fan . . . [but] as a young girl I became very interested [in] and enamored of the Yankees."[18] The teams were in two different leagues, she explained, so she rooted for them both.

Hillary's ideas to revitalize the state of New York eventually won over voters. On November 7, 2000, she easily defeated Lazio. On January 3, 2001, she took office as a United States senator from New York. A little more than two weeks later, her husband completed his second and final term as president of the United States. The couple's roles had shifted: Hillary no longer was a First Lady. She was the elected official. It was Bill's turn to support his wife's political career.

CHAPTER EIGHT

Senator Clinton

· ·

Despite numerous accomplishments, the Clinton years had been marred by scandal, and the Clintons' reputations suffered. This was perhaps unfair for Hillary, who never faced any formal charges of wrongdoing. Nonetheless, there was now a Republican in the White House, and Hillary's political future as a US senator began on less than solid footing.

Her new job was to represent the people of New York. Part of her responsibility was writing and voting on bills. Senators decide whether to vote for or against every bill that comes before Congress. All bills must pass the Senate and the House of Representatives before they can go to the president to be signed into law. Senators can also write their own bills. Then, they work to get the other senators to vote their bills into law. Hillary Clinton went right to work doing that. She introduced bills that would help the people who elected her. Because she was a former First Lady, Clinton was by far the best known of all the senators, but since it was her first term, she

The Legislative Branch

The Senate is one of two branches of the United States Congress. The other is the House of Representatives. The Senate has one hundred members, two from each of the fifty states. The House of Representatives has four hundred thirty-five members because each state receives a certain number of representatives based on its population. Members of both branches work in Washington, DC, as representatives of the people of their state. Both the House of Representatives and in Senate write and vote on bills. If a bill passes both branches, it moves to the president to be signed into law. The president can also veto a bill, stopping it from becoming law. That is, unless Congress votes to override the veto.

did not have a lot of power. She sat on the Environment and Public Works Committee; the Health, Labor, and Pensions Committee; and the Armed Services Committee.

Chelsea Clinton graduated from Stanford University the same year her mother took office. She then moved to England to study international relations at Oxford University. Her father had also studied there. As daughter of a former president, and now of a well-known senator, Chelsea reluctantly remained in the public eye.

Hillary's transition from First Lady to senator began smoothly. New York was prospering. Hillary was learning the ropes of her new job. Everything was going well. But, one late-summer morning, much changed for New York, the United States, and the rest of the world.

Clinton's 9/11

On September 11, 2001, terrorists hijacked four planes loaded with fuel and passengers and crashed them. In all, nearly three thousand people died. Fear and panic filled the country. It was soon discovered that a terrorist organization named al-Qaeda was responsible. That discovery did little to ease people's minds and did nothing to fix the damage that had been done. New York City, where two planes were flown into the World Trade Center towers, looked like an enemy had bombed it. In truth, it had.

Like most Americans, Hillary Clinton watched on television as the tragedy unfolded. In the days and months following the deadliest attack ever in the United States, Senator Clinton sought funding to help her new state rebuild. She and New York's other senator, Charles Schumer, met with President George W. Bush to ask him for more money than he had pledged to give their state. The Republican president immediately said "yes."[1] Hillary said she became teary-eyed at his decision.[2] Later, she said how pleased she was that the country was not worried about whether someone was a Republican or Democrat when it came to this situation. She even teamed with political rivals to accomplish the task. In particular, she was happy she and New York mayor Rudy Giuliani were able to work together to help the country. She told one newspaper, "We're all New Yorkers now. I think we were all victimized by this. There couldn't have been a city anywhere in the

One day after the September 11 attacks, Hillary Clinton, then a US senator from New York, visited ground zero wearing a surgical mask for protection. She later secured $20 billion in federal aid from President George W. Bush.

world that responded with more grit, resolve and just plain guts as New York did. That makes me proud every time I go and speak about it."[3]

Hillary's post-9/11 efforts helped businesses and the families of victims recover. She even attended the funerals of some victims to offer her condolences.

Shortly after 9/11, the United States retaliated against its attackers. President Bush declared a war on terror. In October, the United States, England, and several other countries joined forces to go to Afghanistan. Their goal was to remove the responsible terrorist group, al-Qaeda, from power and capture its leader, Osama bin Laden. This would not happen until many years later, in 2011, when Operation Neptune Spear raided bin Laden's Pakistan compound, killing him and several others present.

> I would meet these shattered lives of people where they were broken, but I saw so many of them strengthen and show such resilience. So I felt privileged. It gave me an insight into the human spirit—and I like to think the spirit of New York and America—that I wish every American could understand. [4]

In 2003, the United States invaded the Middle Eastern country of Iraq, after President Bush said there was evidence that country was building "weapons of mass destruction." Those weapons, he said, could be used to stage another terrorist attack on the United States or elsewhere.

80

Weapons of mass destruction include nuclear and chemical weapons that could kill large numbers of people.

Given the president's reasoning, Senator Clinton voted to wage war on Iraq. At the end of 2003, Iraq's president, Saddam Hussein, was captured. He was put on trial for previous war crimes and executed in 2006. But the United States military never found any weapons of mass destruction. This caused a large number of Americans, including Hillary Clinton, to believe the war was not a good idea, after all.

Senator Clinton and many others also began to disagree with the way the war was being handled. Soon, Clinton began to speak out against the war. In 2007, she led a charge to call another vote on whether the war should continue and if the president should have to get the consent of Congress to continue. She said, "If the president will not bring himself to accept reality, it is time for Congress to bring reality to him."[5] No such vote took place.

Clinton's rivals attacked and accused her of only doing what she thought was best for her political career. They said that when waging war was popular, Clinton was for it. When it was no longer popular, she was against it. She, of course, said that was not true.

Presidential Plans

In 2006, Hillary Clinton was reelected to the Senate, overwhelming her Republican opponent, John Spencer. She gained 67 percent of the vote. The next year, she did something many had long believed she would. She announced she was going to run for president of the United

States. Immediately, she built a team of assistants and began campaigning for the Democratic Party's nomination. Her closest competitor in early polls was Illinois senator Barack Obama. Obama emerged as a popular figure, due in part to his charisma and his popular books.

As the candidates debated and campaigned, Hillary Clinton became the early front-runner. Powerful politicians and financial donors began to pledge support to her campaign. A poll conducted in August 2007 showed 49 percent of voters in the state of California said they planned to vote for Clinton in the Democratic primary.[6] Only 19 percent said they would vote for Obama.[7] Results generally

Although they had been bitter opponents during the 2008 campaign for the Democratic nomination, Hillary Clinton and Barack Obama stood side by side at the State Department shortly after Obama's inauguration in 2009.

are closer in national polls. But, even in those, Hillary Clinton led nearly every time.

In the first of two crushing presidential upsets for Clinton, the 2008 Democratic Party nomination went to Barack Obama. In November, Obama and his running mate Joe Biden went on to victory, soundly defeating the Republican ticket of John McCain and Sarah Palin. As the forty-fourth president of the United States, Obama became the first African American to ever hold the highest office in the land.

As much as women's status in society has risen, there still are many who are not comfortable with a woman as a presidential nominee. Not surprisingly, according to one 2007 poll, women supported Clinton more strongly than men did.[8] The same poll showed Obama was supported equally by both women and men.[9] Clinton knew she would have to fight gender bias. She said, "I'm proud to be running to be the first woman president, but I'm not running because I'm a woman. I'm running because I think I'm the best qualified and experienced to hit the ground running and get the job done."[10]

At least one person saw the possibility of her candidacy as far back as the spring of 1969, when the strong-willed young woman from a small town in Illinois delivered an inspirational graduation speech. After the powerful speech, a classmate had predicted that Hillary Clinton would be president of the United States one day. Though the presidency eluded her in 2008, Clinton's next four years in politics would be far from uneventful. In 2009, Barack Obama appointed Hillary Clinton to a top position in his cabinet: secretary of state.

CHAPTER NINE

State Department

· ·

The Department of State is the federal agency charged with organizing and overseeing US foreign policy. Employees of the State Department work in over 270 locations all over the globe. Its domestic headquarters are in the Harry S. Truman Building, located in Washington, DC. According to its official literature, the Department of State is "responsible for promoting peace and stability in areas of vital interest to America, and helping developing nations establish stable economic environments."[1]

At the helm of this organization is the secretary of state. This is a very powerful position in the president's cabinet. In addition to being the highest-ranking US foreign official, the secretary of state is fourth in the line of succession to the presidency. In the unlikely event that the president, vice president, and Speaker of the House are all incapacitated or otherwise unable to serve, the secretary of state assumes the highest office in the country. It is not an appointment to be taken lightly.

On November 14, 2008, it became public knowledge that President-elect Barack Obama wanted Hillary Clinton to be secretary of state. It was an unexpected choice. The two had just endured an extended, often bitter battle for the Democratic nomination, wherein Obama had openly questioned Clinton's foreign policy qualifications, experience, and judgment. In particular, Obama took Clinton to task for her initial vote in favor of the Iraq War, which was now deeply unpopular and widely viewed as a failure by the American public. As an incoming president however, Obama sought to emulate Abraham Lincoln and assemble a "team of rivals."[2] Clinton certainly fit the bill.

> **At the end of the day, when your president asks you to serve, you say yes, if you can.**

A few days after the election, Hillary and Bill were taking a walk together in a nature preserve near their home in Westchester County, New York. Bill's phone rang, and to Hillary's mild annoyance, he took a business call in this quiet and serene park environment. President-Elect Obama was on the other end. He claimed that he wanted to talk to the former president in general terms about some people he was considering for positions in his administration. Perhaps sensing Obama's intentions, Bill soon passed the phone to his wife. Hillary attests to being somewhat surprised by the offer. She recalled the conversation for Politico: "He said I want you to be my Secretary of State. And I said, 'Oh, no, you don't…there's so many other people who could do this.'"[3]

Hillary quickly accepted. Framing her decision as a matter of patriotic duty rather than politics and career advancement, she claimed, "You know, I'm pretty old-fashioned, and it's just who I am. So at the end of the day, when your president asks you to serve, you say yes, if you can."[4] In addition to being old-fashioned, Hillary was also an astute negotiator. Prior to accepting the post, she insisted Obama ensure that all of her conditions about taking the job, including concerns about access to the president, authority to pick her own staff, and

On May 1, 2011, Secretary of State Clinton, President Obama, Vice President Biden, and others on the national security team received confirmation that a mission to kill Osama bin Laden was successful.

autonomy over policy directions, would be met.[5] The former First Lady was determined to take on the new challenges of the State Department on her own terms. Once she was convinced that she would have sufficient leeway in the job, the choice to accept her new role became much easier.

Still, much would have to be sacrificed. As a senator, Clinton was popular with her constituents, and as a presidential candidate she had amassed 18 million votes. Giving up a Senate seat and subordinating her goals to the Obama agenda would require her to abandon some measure of political independence. Close associates such as former Clinton administration commerce secretary Mickey Kantor insisted this would come naturally to Clinton, who was widely regarded as a "good team player and terrific lawyer," as well as a shrewd, career-minded politician.[6] On foreign policy, Clinton was somewhat to the right of the Obama-Biden team, particularly in the Middle East. For example, Clinton supported classifying Iran's Revolutionary Guard Corps as a foreign terrorist organization, a distinction Obama opposed. In addition, Clinton was a much stauncher and more unilateral supporter of Israel than Obama. Whether these disagreements would form a wedge between her and the president remained to be seen.

By a vote of 94-2, the senate formally confirmed Clinton as the sixty-seventh US secretary of state on January 21, 2009. Her first few months were spent hiring a staff and familiarizing herself with how the State Department runs. Next, she secured a nearly 10% budget increase for her department.[7] Clinton would need the resources—she was inheriting intense fallout from two problematic wars begun under George W. Bush: Iraq and Afghanistan. These significantly undermined US leadership on the world stage, so part of her job as the new secretary of state would be to restore lost order and credibility and to rehabilitate the United States' reputation internationally.

Clinton's approach and skill set fit this mission well, at least initially. Rather than plunge headlong into diplomatic negotiations with potentially hostile heads of state, an approach Obama believed in but Clinton had formerly dismissed as "irresponsible and frankly naïve," Clinton chose instead to leverage foreign aid money toward investment and economic development.[8] She believed that alongside traditional diplomacy, this was the most effective way to advance human rights and US objectives abroad. Though development primarily benefits large multinational corporations first, Clinton always felt this was the most pragmatic way to advance a progressive social agenda. The belief system extolling the social benefits of free trade, competition, and unrestricted movement of capital is often called neoliberalism. Clinton's unflinching adherence to neoliberalism would eventually earn her many detractors from both the political left and right.

To counter criticisms of neoliberal corporatism, it must be said that as secretary of state, Clinton continued to prioritize the global needs of women and children, as she had throughout her political career. An early initiative of hers titled *Quadrennial Diplomacy and Development Review* specified that women's rights and violence against women worldwide should be considered a matter of national security. The document mentioned women and girls 133 times.[9] She also worked hard to fight hunger, championing food security as vital to worldwide stability. A signature move of hers was to introduce millions of modern cookstoves to the developing world. These helped the environment and reduced women's everyday exposure to harmful smoke.

The Arab Spring

World events would conspire to make the second half of Clinton's term a tremendous challenge. The Arab Spring, a series of nonviolent protests against repressive governments across the Middle East and North Africa beginning in Tunisia, caught fire in 2010. Soon massive protests against Egyptian president Hosni Mubarak would place the United States in a bind. On one hand, Mubarak's government was losing legitimacy. It shut down social media sites and even resorted to violence against protesters. On the other hand, Mubarak was a longtime ally, and as America had grown weary of regime change, Obama was reticent to undermine Mubarak's leadership and a sovereign foreign government. As Obama and Clinton waffled somewhat on an official position, the president leaned heavily on Clinton. As a former First Lady herself, Clinton had a good relationship with the Egyptian First Lady and was to some degree trusted. Clinton sent an emissary urging Mubarak not to seek reelection. That would not be necessary. The Egyptian Revolution of 2011 forced him out of power within months.

Libya and Benghazi

Next, civil war broke out in Libya. This time, Clinton was quick to take a position. She said, "Muammar Gaddafi must go now, without further violence or delay."[10] It was unusual for her to take such a firm stand. US policy in the Middle East was a muddle, sometimes backing repressive regimes, other times supporting protesters, and often with little discernable reason or consistency. Clinton immediately called for a no-fly zone and then pushed for an international coalition to bomb the country, killing its leader. This would have serious repercussions. The loss of leadership plunged Libya deeper into civil war, making it a failed state. Unlike its relatively stable neighbor Tunisia, Libya quickly became a haven for extremists such as ISIS. In addition, the ensuing chaos required many to flee the country, sparking a refugee crisis. Finally, there would be violent blowback, affecting Clinton personally.

On September 11, 2012, there was an attack on two US government facilities in Benghazi, Libya. Several Americans died, including US ambassador to Libya J. Christopher Stevens. The Islamic group Ansar Al-Sharia claimed responsibility, though many Libyans, including the prime minister condemned the attacks. Questions remained however: was this a spontaneous

> I take responsibility. I'm in charge of the State Department's 60,000-plus people all over the world, 275 posts ... I take this very personally.

Clinton took full responsibility for the attack on the US Embassy in Benghazi, Libya, that resulted in the death of a US ambassador. Her testimony before the House Select Committee on Benghazi on October 22, 2015, lasted eleven hours.

• • • • • • • • • • • • • • • • • • • •

protest or a planned attack? The CIA, who had been operating on the ground in Benghazi and wished to cover up an intelligence failure, blamed the attack on spontaneous anger arising from an anti-Islamic video called *Innocence of Muslims.* Clinton and the CIA considered the plausibility of this soon to be proven false explanation, but Clinton never officially endorsed it on the public record.

The State Department was heavily criticized for denying requests for additional security at the embassy in Libya. Understandably, the event was a serious blow to Clinton, and she held herself accountable,

Email Controversy

To far too many Americans, the word "email" in the same sentence as "Hillary Clinton" invokes scandal, though few understand what the issue is about. Shortly before she became secretary of state, Clinton set up a private email server in her home in Chappaqua, NY. A server is simply a centralized powerful computer accessible to a network. State officials generally use US–government hosted servers, so the server was unusual, though not illegal. Clinton insisted that protecting the privacy of emails was her prerogative because the emails were often of a personal nature, in addition to work. She came under repeated fire during the 2016 election for this when opponents suggested Clinton had deleted emails to cover up wrongdoing, possibly connected to Benghazi, another favorite buzzword for Clinton's opponents. No ethical or legal breaches were ever proven, but a last-minute investigation (quickly dropped) by FBI head James Comey further sullied Clinton's reputation and hurt her going into the election. Ironically, the Trump administration immediately followed suit, establishing private servers for many key officials.

stating, "I take responsibility. I'm in charge of the State Department's 60,000-plus people all over the world, 275 posts ... I take this very personally."[11] When Obama won reelection in November, Clinton announced that she would only remain secretary of state until a successor was named.

Clinton left the post with a mixed legacy. Her contribution to women's health, human rights, and economic development abroad was universally lauded, but failure in Libya perhaps unfairly fell mostly on her shoulders. Obama confessed doubts about the intervention, claiming it was Clinton's idea, though as commander in chief, it was ultimately his call. To this day, Clinton defends the Libyan intervention, saying it helped avoid a brutal civil war of the kind currently raging in Syria. Regardless of who is right, the political cost for Clinton was enormous. She may have underestimated this—after recovering from health issues, she wasted little time planning another presidential run for 2016.

CHAPTER TEN

Another Run

· · · · · · · · · · · · · · · · · · · ·

Hillary Clinton announced her intention to run for president again in 2016 on YouTube. The video, which received just shy of 1,000,000 views, features a montage of ordinary Americans talking candidly about their diverse lives, work, and ambitions: a middle-aged rural woman boasts of her "legendary" homegrown tomatoes, two brothers discuss starting a small business (in Spanish with subtitles), a young Asian American woman who just graduated from college is nervous about job prospects and paying off student loans, a same-sex couple looks forward to an upcoming summer wedding, a single mom is moving her daughter to a better school district, a retiree talks about personal reinvention.[1] The final person is a white, blue-collar male engaged in manual labor, representative of the important "rust belt" demographic Clinton desperately needed but failed to court. He claims that he's starting a new career at a fifth-generation-owned company, and that "America is built on hard work."[2]

About a minute and a half into the two-and-a-half-minute video, Hillary Clinton finally appears on camera. Like those who preceded her, she too is ready for a new challenge, mentioning conversationally, "I'm getting ready to do something too. I'm running for president." Clinton then echoes a sentiment we'd often hear on the campaign trail, though generally more from her Democratic challenger Bernie Sanders, that "the deck is still stacked in favor of those at the top."[3]

Clinton's announcement video is an effective, and in retrospect, particularly to those who voted for her, heartbreaking attempt to align her campaign with paradigmatic liberal themes of diversity, economic equality, and social justice. The video acknowledges the generalized anxiety of economic hardship, which cut across various societal dividing lines such as race, class, gender, and sexuality. Many felt left behind and forgotten by the supposed economic recovery of the Obama years, which tended to benefit top earners, especially those in the financial services sector, the most. Though not often credited as such, Clinton spoke to these concerns from day one. For many reasons, her message did not connect with and mobilize enough voters to win. Still, the contrast between her platform and that of her Republican opponent could not have been more diametrically opposed.

> "I'm getting ready to do something too. I'm running for president."

Clinton shook hands with supporters at the Women for Hillary Kick-off in Portsmouth, New Hampshire, on September 5, 2015. In a major upset, Bernie Sanders, senator of neighboring Vermont, won the state primary by a large margin.

Descending down a gold elevator in Trump Tower, flanked by his wife, Melania, a former model dressed in white leather designer garb, the man who would defeat Clinton and become the forty-fifth president of the United States had some contrasting points to make. In his announcement speech, Donald Trump fixated on a tragic, though largely imaginary, sense of lost national glory and incited fear of and racist hatred for groups often coded as "other," such as immigrants and Muslims. Trump complained multiple times about bad trade deals with China, the United States' failure to defeat ISIS, and the need to secure international borders. Speaking about Mexico, Trump infamously observed, "they're sending people that have lots of problems, and they're bringing those problems with us. They're bringing drugs. They're bringing crime. They're rapists."[4] In a speech that was equal parts populist chicanery and xenophobic demagoguery, Donald Trump staked his claim to the Republican Party's nomination for president on hostile negative impulses from day one. In a historically weak crop of Republican hopefuls, Trump said whatever was necessary to easily defeat his closest rivals, including Jeb Bush, Marco Rubio, Ted Cruz, and John Kasich.

On paper, the general election should have been no contest. Hillary Clinton was easily the most qualified candidate in either party's 2016 field. At the Democratic National Convention in Philadelphia, Barack Obama unequivocally endorsed Clinton, saying, "There has never been a man or a woman, not me, not Bill [Clinton], nobody more qualified than Hillary Clinton

On July 28, 2016, Clinton took the stage at the Democratic National Convention in Philadelphia to accept the party nomination. With this, Hillary Clinton became the first female presidential nominee from either major US political party.

to serve as president of the United States of America."[5] By contrast, her challenger was a New York City real estate developer and reality television personality who had never held an elected office, well known for his catchphrase "You're fired!" and his casual misogyny, racism, and xenophobia.

While it was open to contestation whether Clinton was truly the most qualified candidate ever to run for president, it was almost unanimous that Trump was definitely the least qualified. Dozens of news organizations including the *New York Times*, *Los Angeles Times*, and even the usually neutral *USA Today* denounced Trump and endorsed Clinton. On July 22 of 2016, the entire editorial staff of the *Washington Post* united to issue an unprecedented statement warning that "Donald Trump is a unique threat to American Democracy."[6] Trump supporters were unfazed. In fact, these repeated warnings only seemed to egg on those inclined to distrust so-called media elites. Plus, all the free advertising boosted Trump's allure as a tempting, dangerous outsider who would shake the Washington, DC, status quo to its core.

Who *were* all these people who wanted a shady businessman and huckster with no prior political experience to hold the most powerful office in the world? Clinton tried to formulate an answer, with terrible results. At a fund-raising event in September 2016, Clinton made the following statement, which was soon seen as a major gaffe: "You know, to just be grossly generalistic, you could put half of Trump's supporters into what I call the basket of deplorables. Right? The racist, sexist, homophobic, xenophobic, Islamophobic, you name it. And unfortunately there are people like that. And he has lifted them up. He has given voice to their websites that used to only have 11,000 people, now have 11 million."[7] Regardless of the veracity of her claim, the phrase "basket of deplorables" quickly backfired on Clinton and was endlessly repeated by her opponents as proof that she too was a liberal elite, out of touch with real Americans.

An Insurgency Within the Democrats

Another challenge came from within the Democratic Party itself. Though technically an independent, Vermont senator Bernie Sanders ran an insurgent campaign to the political left of Clinton on many important economic and social issues, earning an enthusiastic grassroots following, particularly among younger voters. The bulk of Sanders's supporters saw Clinton as too entrenched in the same political and corporate status quo their candidate railed against. Her penchant for accepting highly paid speaking engagements from patrons such as Goldman Sachs especially rankled the "Sandernistas." To Clinton's defense, Wall Street comprises a large percentage of New York State's gross domestic product (GDP). As a senator, it would have been unwise to alienate the financial services industry, tantamount to a California senator ignoring Silicon Valley. As for her six-figure speaking fees, these were not unusual for people of her stature, though these people were usually men.

The internal critique from the Sanders camp sowed party disunity, which hurt Clinton in November.

Although Clinton won both the popular and electoral votes in the Democratic primaries, a suggestion that the Democratic National Committee "rigged" the process against Sanders haunted Clinton. A vocal faction of Democrats took up the extreme position of "Bernie or bust" and refused to back Clinton. Some even defected to the Republican candidate. Third party challengers Jill Stein and Gary Johnson peeled away two million votes. The majority of these would

Should We Abolish the Electoral College?

The Electoral College consists of 538 electors. In December, little over a month after the general election, these men and women convene to actually elect the president of the United States. The system was created at the founding of the nation and is written into the Constitution. Critics counter that it violates the "one person one vote" principle essential to democracy. Moreover, it was created in the past when campaign activity tended to be concentrated in populated areas. Mass media now makes the geographic factor less relevant. Defenders of the Electoral College argue that candidates should have a wide geographic appeal. If a candidate won only cities and had no appeal to rural voters, it would be unfair to less populated states. Currently, the electorate is more divided between urban and rural areas than ever. This is likely to stay the case regardless of the eventual fate of the Electoral College.

have gone for Clinton, though these voters were heavily concentrated in states she already won.

On November 8, 2016, Clinton won the popular vote by over three million votes. She did not become president. Owing to the Electoral College, an arcane institution that gives disproportionate power to sparsely populated rural states in the traditionally conservative heartland, Trump received 306 Electoral College votes to Clinton's 232. It was one of greatest political upsets in history. Many found it difficult to process, a kind of grieving. David Remnick of the *New Yorker* wrote, "The election of Donald Trump to the Presidency is nothing less than a tragedy for the American republic, a tragedy for the Constitution, and a triumph for the forces, at home and abroad, of nativism, authoritarianism, misogyny, and racism."[8]

> "To all the little girls watching...never doubt that you are valuable and powerful and deserving of every chance and opportunity in the world."

American Tragedy

In the aftermath of the election, countless pundits and observers attempted to make sense of the results, analyzing voter demographics in minute detail. Was it that Clinton could not connect with evangelicals? Did her position on late-term abortion alienate Catholics? Some plausibly suggested she didn't campaign hard enough in the rust belt and thus failed to win over the "Obama coalition" of working class whites, blacks, and Latinos. Surely sexism was a factor,

Clinton's loss compelled many to wonder if America would ever be ready for a woman president. She has said that "the advancement of the full participation of women and girls in every aspect of their societies is the great unfinished business of the 21st century."

• • • • • • • • • • • • • • • • • • • •

but this is difficult to quantify and measure. Still others clung to a theory of malevolent foreign interference. The Democratic establishment asserted that operatives close to Russian president Vladimir Putin leaked emails that hurt Clinton in the home stretch. Was it possible that a foreign government installed Trump as a "Manchurian candidate"? Perhaps, but no smoking gun linking Trump's victory to Russian interference surfaced.

Conspiracies aside, the most plausible explanation behind Clinton's loss was simple: low voter turnout. Given the choice between Trump and Clinton, more than ninety million Americans chose to stay home. A distressing number of young voters saw the contest of Clinton vs. Trump as the lesser of two evils. This position is confounding, given the vast gulf separating their qualifications and values. Superficially however, many saw two elderly, rich, white establishment figures and intuited that neither would meaningfully represent their interests. Perhaps they were not entirely wrong; all Western democracies have been moving away from globalism, and the Clintons were the primary architects of this paradigm.

In her concession speech, Clinton reiterated her efforts on behalf of women and girls everywhere: "To all the little girls watching...never doubt that you are valuable and powerful and deserving of every chance and opportunity in the world."[9]

Hillary Clinton would not shatter the glass ceiling barring women from the presidency. She had the great misfortune of running in a heavily antiestablishment climate when the Clinton brand of centrist liberalism was no match for peoples' hunger for "change," for better or for worse. Nonetheless, Hillary Clinton got closer than any woman has yet, and her name will certainly be remembered once this remnant of historical sexism is finally overcome.

Chronology

1947 Hillary Diane Rodham born on October 26 in Chicago, Illinois, to Hugh and Dorothy Rodham. Lives with family in one-bedroom apartment.

1950 Moves with family to Chicago suburb of Park Ridge, Illinois; father commutes to Chicago for work, mother stays at home to take care of family; brother Hugh born.

1954 Brother Anthony born.

1960 Helps Republicans investigate voter addresses after Democrat John F. Kennedy wins presidency; gets first summer job working for the Park Ridge Park District.

1961 Writes letter to NASA saying she would like to be an astronaut; NASA responds by saying females are not accepted into its space program.

1963 Hears speech given by civil rights activist Dr. Martin Luther King Jr. in Chicago.

1964 Joins Young Republicans; campaigns for Barry Goldwater in his run for the presidency.

1965 Moves to Wellesley, Massachusetts, to begin freshman year at Wellesley College, an all-female school; initially struggles to adapt; elected president of Young Republicans.

1966 Resigns Young Republicans post; becomes Democrat.

1968 Campaigns for Eugene McCarthy, who is seeking the Democratic Party's nomination for president; interns in Washington, DC, for a Republican congressman; attends Republican National Convention in Miami to help Nelson Rockefeller gain the Republican presidential nomination; attends Democratic National Convention in Chicago; elected president of Wellesley's senior class.

1969 Becomes first-ever student graduation speaker at Wellesley; upstages a US senator with speech and gains nationally notoriety for doing so; graduates from Wellesley; moves to New Haven, Connecticut, to attend Yale Law School.

1970 Meets Marian Wright Edelman; interns with Edelman working on children's issues in Washington, DC; meets fellow law school student Bill Clinton.

1971 Begins dating Bill Clinton; moves into apartment with Clinton.

1972 Moves with Bill Clinton to Texas for summer to work on Democrat George McGovern's presidential campaign; spends a fourth year at Yale Law School working on children's issues

1973 Graduates, with Bill Clinton, from Yale Law School; rejects Clinton's marriage proposal; moves to Massachusetts to work as attorney for the Children's Defense Fund.

1974 Moves to Washington, DC, to work on impeachment case against President Richard Nixon; takes teaching job at University of Arkansas; helps Clinton run for US House of Representatives.

1975 Marries Bill Clinton on October 11.

1976 Helps Clinton get elected as attorney general of Arkansas; moves to Little Rock; begins work for Rose Law Firm.

1979 Becomes First Lady of Arkansas when Clinton is elected state governor.

1980 Gives birth to Chelsea Victoria Clinton on February 27; husband loses reelection bid.

1982 Decides to change name from Hillary Rodham to Hillary Rodham Clinton; husband wins election and again serves as Arkansas governor.

1983 Leads Arkansas Education Standards Committee.

1984 Named Arkansas Woman of the Year by a newspaper.

1992 Responds publicly to allegations of Bill's womanizing; helps Bill Clinton get elected forty-second president of the United States.

1993 Moves with family into White House; becomes America's First Lady; heads national health care reform task force; father dies on April 7; Whitewater controversy surfaces; gets wrapped up in Travelgate controversy.

1996 Publishes *It Takes a Village and Other Lessons Children Teach Us*; embarks on cross-country book tour.

1997 *It Takes a Village* wins Grammy Award for Best Spoken Word Album; begins traveling to other countries as a United States spokesperson.

1998 Bill Clinton admits to an affair with White House intern Monica Lewinsky; Clinton impeached.

2000 Moves to New York; elected to United States Senate.

2001 Nearly three thousand people die when hijacked planes crash into the World Trade Center towers in New York City, the Pentagon in Washington, DC, and a field in Pennsylvania on September 11; secures additional funding to help New York State's recovery.

2002 Votes to allow president to wage war on Iraq.

2003 Publishes autobiography, *Living History*.

2006 Reelected to Senate.

2007 Announces decision to run for president in 2008.

2008 Concedes defeat to Barack Obama to secure the Democratic nomination for president.

2009 Becomes secretary of state in Obama's administration.

2011 Osama bin Laden raids: Clinton is a key player in the operation that killed bin Laden.

2012 US Embassy in Bengazi attacked by Libya; State Department and Clinton heavily criticized about the Bengazi attack.

2013 Steps down as secretary of state.

2014 Hillary Clinton cleared over any wrongdoing regarding the Bengazi attack.

2015 Private email controversy breaks just as Clinton decides to run for president.

2016 Clinton wins Democratic primaries against Bernie Sanders, becoming the first US woman to run as a major party presidential nominee. Clinton wins the national popular vote but loses the Electoral College vote, conceding the presidency to Republican Donald Trump.

Chapter Notes

Chapter 1. Graduation Speech

1. Wellesley College 1969 Student Commencement Speech, July 19, 1999, http://www.wellesley.edu/PublicAffairs/Commencement/1969/053169hillary.html (March 27, 2007).

2. Wellesley College Commencement Address 1969 Senator Edward W. Brooke, July 15, 1999, http://www.wellesley.edu/PublicAffairs/Commencement/1969/brooke.html (March 27, 2007).

3. Ibid.

4. Ibid.

5. Donnie Radcliffe, *A First Lady for Our Time* (New York, NY: Warner Books, 1993), p. 81.

6. Wellesley College 1969 Student Commencement Speech.

7. Radcliffe, p. 81.

8. Wellesley College 1969 Student Commencement Speech.

9. Ibid.

10. Ibid.

11. *Frontline*, "Hillary's Class," PBS.org, http://www.pbs.org/wgbh/pages/frontline/twenty/watch/hillary.html (May 14, 2007).

12. Ibid.

13. Ibid.

Chapter 2. Early Years

1. Howard B. Furer, *Chicago: A Chronological and Documentary History* (Dobbs Ferry, NY: Oceana Publications, 1974), p. 19.

2. Chicago Timeline, "1833 Incorporated as a Town— Origin of Name," Chicago Public Library, August 1997, http://www.chipublib.org/004chicago/timeline/originame.html (March 15, 2007).

3. Furer, p. 33.

4. Chicago Timeline. "Population of Chicago by Decades 1830–2000," Chicago Public Library, April 2001, http://www.chipublib.org/004chicago/timeline/population.html (March 30, 2007).

5. Hillary Rodham Clinton, *Living History* (New York, NY: Scribner, 2003), p. 9.

6. Hillaryclinton.com, "Growing Up in Illinois," http://www.hillaryclinton.com/about/growingup/ (April 1, 2007).

7. Hillary Rodham Clinton, *It Takes a Village and Other Lessons Children Teach Us* (New York, NY: Simon and Schuster, 1996), p. 23.

8. Ibid., p. 22.

9. Ibid.

10. Claire G. Osborne, ed., *Hillary Rodham Clinton: A Portrait in Her Own Words* (New York, NY: Avon Books, 1997), p. 3.

11. Ibid.

12. Clinton, *It Takes a Village and Other Lessons Children Teach Us*, p. 22.

13. Ibid.

14. Clinton, *Living History*, p. 17.

15. Ibid.

16. Ibid., p. 12.

17. Associated Press, "Women's Hall of Fame Honors Hillary Clinton, 9 Others," *USA Today*, October 9, 2005, http://www.usatoday.com/news/washington/2005-10-09-women-clinton_x.htm (April 17, 2007).

18. Clinton, *It Takes a Village and Other Lessons Children Teach Us*, p. 27.

19. Hillary for President, "Civil Rights: On the 42nd Anniversary of Bloody Sunday in Selma," http://www.hillaryclinton.com/news/speech/view/?id=1362 (March 30, 2007).

20. Clinton, *Living History*, p. 21.

21. Osborne, p. 8.

22. Clinton, *Living History*, p. 25.

Chapter 3. Class President

1. Claire G. Osborne, ed., *Hillary Rodham Clinton: A Portrait in Her Own Words* (New York, NY: Avon Books, 1997), p. 9.

2. Donnie Radcliffe, *A First Lady for Our Time* (New York, NY: Warner Books, 1993), p. 57.

3. Hillary Rodham Clinton, *Living History* (New York, NY: Scribner, 2003), p. 27.

4. Ibid., p. 31.

5. David L. Anderson, *The Columbia Guide to the Vietnam War* (New York, NY: Columbia University Press, 2002), p. 78.

6. Ibid.

7. Clinton, *Living History*, p. 31.

8. Radcliffe, p. 73.

9. Joyce Milton, *The First Partner: Hillary Rodham Clinton* (New York, NY: Perennial, 2000), p. 31

10. Clinton, *Living History*, p. 37.

11. Radcliffe, pp. 74–75.

12. Osborne, p. 10.

13. Ben Norton, "Hillary Clinton Lost Sleep Trying to Talk Wellesley Students Out of Vietnam War Protests," Salon.com, November 4, 2016. http://www.salon.com/2016/11/04/hillary-clinton-lost-sleep-trying-to-talk-wellesley-students-out-of-vietnam-war-protests/.

14. Radcliffe, p. 80.

15. Clinton, *Living History*, p. 40.

16. Radcliffe, p. 82.

17. Clinton, *Living History*, p. 42.

18. Ibid., p. 43.

Chapter 4. Rodham Meets Clinton

1. Hillary Rodham Clinton, *Living History* (New York, NY: Scribner, 2003), pp. 45–46.

2. Claire G. Osborne, ed., *Hillary Rodham Clinton: A Portrait in Her Own Words* (New York, NY: Avon Books, 1997), p. 14.

3. Bill Clinton, *My Life* (New York, NY: Alfred A. Knopf, 2004), p. 181.

4. Ibid., p. 182.

5. Ibid., p. 20.

6. Clinton, *Living History*, p. 61.

7. Ibid., p. 64.

8. Ibid., p. 70.

9. Bill Clinton, *My Life*, p. 233.

10. Joyce Milton, *The First Partner: Hillary Rodham Clinton* (New York, NY: Perennial, 2000), p. 102.

11. Clinton, *Living History*, p. 81.

Chapter 5. Governor's Mansion

1. Hillary Rodham Clinton, *Living History* (New York, NY: Scribner, 2003), p. 91.

2. Ibid.

3. Claire G. Osborne, ed., *Hillary Rodham Clinton: A Portrait in Her Own Words* (New York, NY: Avon Books, 1997), pp. 20–21.

4. Osborne, p. 51.

5. Ibid., p. 72

6. Bill Clinton, "Announcement Speech," October 3, 1991, 4president.org, http://www.4president.org/speeches/billclinton1992announcement.htm (May 14, 2007).

7. Osborne, p. 37.

Chapter 6. Road to Washington

1. Claire G. Osborne, ed., *Hillary Rodham Clinton: A Portrait in Her Own Words* (New York, NY: Avon Books, 1997), p. 52

2. Ibid.

3. Joyce Milton, *The First Partner: Hillary Rodham Clinton* (New York, NY: Perennial, 2000), p. 220.

4. Ibid., p. 221.

5. Osborne, p. 47.

6. Clinton, *Living History*, p. 113.

7. Ibid., p. 117.

8. Ibid., p. 119.

Chapter 7. First Couple

1. Bill Clinton's First Inaugural Address, January 21, 1993, Bartleby.com, http://www.bartleby.com/124/pres64.Html (April 23, 2007).

2. Hillary Rodham Clinton, *Living History* (New York, NY: Scribner, 2003), p. 125.

3. WhiteHouse.gov, "White House Facts," http://www.whitehouse.gov/history/facts.html (May 15, 2007).

4. Clinton, *Living History*, p. 132.

5. Osborne, p. 148.

6. Clinton, *Living History*, pp. 163–164.

7. Osborne, p. 133.

8. Ibid.

9. Osborne, p. 138.

10. Ibid., p. 172.

11. Cristina Silva, "Hillary Clinton Quotes: 40 of the Best Sayings from the Democratic Presidential Candidate," *International Business Times*, September 24, 2016. http://www.ibtimes.com/hillary-clinton-quotes-40-best-sayings-democratic-presidential-candidate-2421462 (February 20, 2017).

12. James Bennet, "The President Under Fire: The First Lady; Rallying the Defense of Her Husband, Again," *New York Times*, January 25, 1998, http://query.nytimes.com/gst/fullpage.html?res=9B07E5DC133BF936A15752C0A96E958260 (May 9, 2007).

13. CNN.com, "Grand Jury Convenes Without Lewinsky Testimony: Mrs. Clinton Says Attack Is a 'Right-Wing Conspiracy,'" January 27, 1998, http://www.cnn.com/ALLPOLITICS/1998/01/27/clinton.main/ (May 10, 2007).

14. Ibid.

15. Clinton, *Living History*, p. 466.

16. Ibid.

17. CNN.com, "President Bill Clinton: August 17, 1998 speech," http://www.cnn.com/ALLPOLITICS/1998/08/17/speech/transcript.html (May 4, 2007).

18. Joyce Milton, *The First Partner: Hillary Rodham Clinton*, (New York, NY: Perennial, 2000), p. 415.

Chapter 8. Senator Clinton

1. David Barstow, "A Nation Challenged: Federal Aid; Old Rivals, but One Voice in Request for Help," *New York Times*, September 19, 2001, http://query.nytimes.com/gst/fullpage.html?res=9E0CE3D9123BF93AA2575AC0A9679C8B63&sec=&spon=&pagewanted=1 (May 9, 2007).

2. Ibid.

3. Jennifer Steinhauer and Raymond Hernandez, "A Nation Challenged: The Mayor; Giuliani and Senator Clinton: Once Rivals, Now Allies," *New York Times*, September 22, 2001, http://query.nytimes.com/gst/fullpage.html?res=9800E7DC163AF931A1575AC0A9679C8B63&sec=&spon=&pagewanted=2 (May 9, 2007).

4. MJ Lee, "Clinton on 9/11: The Closest Thing to 'Hell' I've Ever Seen," CNN.com, September 11, 2016. http://www.cnn.com/2016/09/11/politics/hillary-clinton-september-11/.

5. Devlin Barrett, "Clinton Seeks New Vote in Authorizing Military Effort in Iraq," Associated Press, May 3, 2007, Newsday.com, http://www.newsday.com/news/local/wire/newyork/ny-bc-ny—clinton-iraq0503may03,0,6761950.story?coll=ny-region-apnewyork (May 10, 2007).

6. Associated Press, "Poll: Nearly Half Favoring Clinton in Calif. Democratic Primary," *San Jose Mercury News*, August 17, 2007, http://www.mercurynews.com/breakingnews/ci_6648360 (August 22, 2007).

7. Ibid.

8. Matt Stearns, "Will U.S. Voters Elect a Woman as President?" *Seattle Times*, August 21, 2007, http://seattletimes.nwsource.com/html/nationworld/2003845865_clinton21.html (August 22, 2007).

9. Ibid.

10. Ibid.

Chapter 9: State Department

1. US Department of State, "What We Do," 2016, https://careers.state.gov/learn/what-we-do.

2. Todd Purdum. "Team of Mascots." *Vanity Fair,* July 2012, http://www.vanityfair.com/news/2012/07/obama-cabinet-team-rivals-lincoln.

3. Andy Barr, "Clinton: I'd Have Hired Obama," *Politico,* October 14, 2009, http://www.politico.com/story/2009/10/clinton-id-have-hired-obama-028278.

4. Ibid.

5. Peter Baker and Helene Cooper, "Clinton Is Said to Accept Secretary of State Position," *New York Times,* November 21, 2008, http://www.nytimes.com/2008/11/22/us/politics/22obama.html.

6. Ibid.

7. Ibid.

8. Healy, Patrick. "Clinton and Obama Campaigns Spar Over Debate," *New York Times,* July 25, 2007, http://www.nytimes.com/2007/07/25/us/politics/25debate.html.

9. US Department of State, "Quadrennial Diplomacy and Development Review," https://www.state.gov/documents/organization/153109.pdf.

10. Andrew Andrew, "Clinton Says Gaddafi Must Go," *Reuters*, February 28, 2011, http://www.reuters.com/article/us-libya-usa-clinton-idUSTRE71Q1JA20110228.

11. Elise Labatt, "Clinton: I'm Responsible for Diplomats' Security," CNN.com, October 16, 2012, http://www.cnn.com/2012/10/15/us/clinton-benghazi/.

Chapter 10: Another Run

1. YouTube, "Hillary Clinton's 2016 Presidential Campaign Announcement," April 12, 2015, https://www.youtube.com/watch?v=N708P-A45D0.

2. Ibid.

3. Ibid.

4. *Time*, "Donald Trump's Announcement Speech," June 16, 2015, http://time.com/3923128/donald-trump-announcement-speech/.

5. Emily Crockett, "Obama: 'Not Me Not Bill Nobody' Has Been More Qualified than Hillary for President,Vox, July 27, 2016, http://www.vox.com/2016/7/27/12306702/democratic-convention-obama-hillary-clinton-bill-qualified.

6. *Washington Post*, "Donald Trump Is a Unique Threat to American Democracy," July 22, 2016, https://www.washingtonpost.com/opinions/donald-trump-is-a-unique-threat-to-american-democracy/2016/07/22/a6d823cc-4f4f-11e6-aa14-e0c1087f7583_story.html?utm_term=.c0ff8adf3a55.

7. *Los Angeles Times,* "Campaign 2016 Updates: Republicans Pounce Upon Clinton 'Deplorables' Remark. She Apologizes. Sort Of," September 10, 2016, http://www.latimes.com/nation/politics/trailguide/la-na-trailguide-updates-transcript-clinton-s-full-remarks-as-1473549076-htmlstory.html.

8. David Remnick, "An American Tragedy," *New Yorker,* November 9, 2016, http://www.newyorker.com/news/news-desk/an-american-tragedy-2.

9. Hillary Clinton, Twitter.com, November 9, 2016, https://twitter.com/hillaryclinton/status/796394920051441664?lang=en.

Glossary

Arab Spring Popular nonviolent uprising against repressive governments in the Middle East and North Africa beginning in 2010.

Benghazi Second most populous city in Libya and site of an attack that killed an American ambassador and others.

Black Panthers Begun in 1966, the Black Panthers was a revolutionary socialist group serving and defending the African American community.

Children's Defense Fund Nonprofit organization formed in 1973 focusing on children's advocacy and research. Hillary Clinton has a longtime association with this group.

Democratic National Committee (DNC) Formal governing body of the US Democratic Party.

glass ceiling Term used to denote unfair and sexist limitations placed on women, minorities, and others excluded from power.

Manchurian Candidate Term taken from the novel and popular movie of the same name to refer to a president controlled by a foreign power.

Rhodes Scholarship World's oldest and highly prestigious fellowship program at Oxford University in the United Kingdom.

Travelgate Ethical inquiry early in Bill Clinton's presidency. Began with the firing of seven members of the White House Travel Office for accounting discrepancies.

Whitewater Political and legal investigation concerning the Clintons' real estate holdings in Arkansas.

Young Republicans Organization for Republicans under the age of forty. Hillary Clinton was a former member.

Further Reading

Books

Clinton, Hillary Rodham. *Hard Choices.* New York, NY: Scribner, 2013.

D'Souza, Dinesh. *Hillary's America.* New York, NY: Regnrey Publishing, 2016.

Ghattas, Kim. *The Secretary: A Journey with Hillary Clinton from Beirut to the Heart of American Power.* New York, NY: Macmillan, 2013

Landler, Mark. *Alter Egos: Hillary Clinton, Barack Obama and the Twilight Struggle Over American Power.* New York, NY: Random House, 2016.

Websites

Biography: Hillary Clinton

www.biography.com/people/hillary-clinton-9251306
A basic biography of the First Lady, senator, and secretary of state.

Hillary Clinton's Senate Voting Record

http://projects.washingtonpost.com/congress/members/C001041/

This page catalogues Clinton's votes while serving in the US Ssenate.

Hillary for President

www.hillaryclinton.com

Hillary Clinton's presidential campaign page.

National First Ladies Library: Hillary Clinton

www.firstladies.org/biographies/firstladies.aspx?biography=43

This site examines Hillary Clinton's accomplishments as First Lady.

Index